THE PHILOSOPHY
OF
THOMAS HILL GREEN

BY
W. H. FAIRBROTHER, M.A.
LECTURER IN PHILOSOPHY AT LINCOLN COLLEGE
OXFORD

SECOND EDITION

METHUEN & CO.
36 ESSEX STREET W.C.
LONDON
1900

Printing Statement:

Due to the very old age and scarcity of this book, many of the pages may be hard to read due to the blurring of the original text, possible missing pages, missing text, dark backgrounds and other issues beyond our control.

Because this is such an important and rare work, we believe it is best to reproduce this book regardless of its original condition.

Thank you for your understanding.

PREFATORY NOTE

THE substance of the following pages was originally given, in the form of lectures, to students of philosophy at Oxford. It has been entirely recast and rewritten, as well as added to, but my object is the same, viz., a simple, plain exposition of the philosophic teaching of T. H. Green. Such an exposition ought to have a certain value of its own, but my real motive is to help the younger student to "read Green" for himself. In the ordinary course of tutorial work it has been found that, to many men, Green is not easy reading. The sterling honesty which made him so anxiously painstaking in writing his sentences, lest they should express more than seemed to him the exact truth, has, for its effect, that the reader experiences something of the same mental effort. Those who felt his personal influence need no further help or stimulus in reading his books, but men who only know Green through his writings, and perhaps, as yet, scarcely realise the importance of the questions under discussion, sometimes find his thorough and exhaustive method of treatment a little too difficult for them. The result is too often a superficial and second-hand acquaintance with his supposed views. The loss is incalculable. Opinions may differ as to the value of Green's conclusions, or even the cogency of his reasoning, but no one can question the benefit to be derived from a thorough study of his teaching. His is, perhaps, the only modern philosophy of life which is, at once, complete and consistent—which derives and justifies both moral responsibility in the present, and hope for the future, from a rigorously scientific metaphysic.

It is solely in the belief that a short, straightforward account of Green's method of working, with the results thereby arrived at, may indirectly help to promote the study of his writings, that these few pages have been written.

LINCOLN COLLEGE, OXFORD,
January, 1896.

CONTENTS

Introductory	9
The Method of Metaphysic	14
The Results of Metaphysic	20
The Freedom of Man	51
Moral Philosophy	58
Political Philosophy	109
Green and his Critics	155

CHAPTER I.

INTRODUCTORY

IF a phrase be sought with which to sum up Professor Green's general position in regard to life and its problems, it would be difficult to find one more fitting than Aristotle's ἐσμὲν ἐνεργείᾳ. Not in wisdom merely, or in potential capacity, but in actually living his life, does Green hold that true well-being for a man is to be found. To discover and to demonstrate in what true human well-being consists is the highest intellectual object for man, and is specially the aim which philosophy should set before itself; to realise this discovery in civic life is the one practical function of the good citizen. Thus Green's primary aim is Moral and Political Philosophy, of which the latter[1] is

---

[1] *Cf.* Works ii. p. 335. "My purpose is to consider the moral function, or object, served by law, or by the system of rights and obligations which the State enforces, and, in so doing, to discover the true ground, or justification, for obedience to law."

Ibid. p. 334. Nettleship's note. Civil institutions are "regarded as the external expression of the moral progress of mankind, and as supplying the material through which the idea of perfection must be realised."

only the application to facts of social life, under definite circumstances, of the truths arrived at by the former.

But before a theory of *Ethics* is possible, a preliminary task must be fulfilled. It is in vain to answer the question, "What ought the good citizen to do?" until the prior question, "What is a citizen, both in himself and in his environment?"[1] has been dealt with. "Some conclusion in regard to the relation between man and nature . . . must be arrived at, before we can be sure that any theory of *Ethics* . . . is other than wasted labour," is Green's explanation of the fact that the first book of his *Ethical Treatise* consists of pure Metaphysics. And Green had a special and pressing necessity for this preliminary inquiry. Current English philosophy seemed to have reduced man to a "being who is simply a result of natural forces,"[2] which, as a necessary consequence, involves the reduction of the theoretical part of Moral Philosophy to a natural science, and the abolition of the practical or preceptive part altogether. A theory of conduct is unmeaning, if conduct itself is impossible; and equally unmeaning is it to bid a being to conform to certain natural laws, if he is simply a result of their operation. A new "Critical Philosophy" is needed, which shall ask,

---

[1] *Proleg. to Ethics*, § 52.
[2] *Proleg.* § 7.

"Is man simply a 'natural' product in this sense?" Can what we call science, *i.e.* the experience of connected matters of fact, be explained, if man is nothing but a number of such matters of fact, or their result? Is there not involved in knowledge a principle which is not[1] "natural," but "spiritual"? These questions must be first settled if our labour, as moralists, is not to be profitless.

Hence, Green's philosophy begins with Metaphysics, and is based entirely upon Metaphysics. It is to this that its entire consistency is due.

As far as possible, without pre-supposition, he carefully, scientifically, thoroughly, reasons out an answer to the question, "What is the nature of man?" From that he deduces his doctrine of man's ἔργον—of what man ought to do, and this, again, he uses as a criterion of the moral progress, or condition, of political society at any time, regarding civic and social institutions as the objective expression of moral ideas, and the concrete body with which the Moral Ideal is to be clothed.

Green's Metaphysical, Moral, and Political Philosophy thus form one whole, and offer a theory of life not only complete, in the sense of covering all the ground, but consistent with itself throughout. More directly, if not more definitely, than, perhaps, in any other modern writer, the whole

[1] *Vide* note at end of chapter.

work stands, or falls, with the metaphysical basis. The first question to ask, then, is what is this Metaphysic—in its method and in its results?

Note on Green's use of the words "natural" *v.* "spiritual." The sense in which Green uses the word "Nature," is that common to ordinary men of science, and to empirical teachers in philosophy, viz.: "The object of possible experience; the connected order of knowable facts or phenomena." This is obviously a very, if not the most, convenient use of a word which, though full of ambiguity, cannot be avoided in philosophic writing. The difference between Green and the Empiricists, and the necessity for employing the word "spiritual," arises as follows:—They use the word "Nature," not only legitimately, as = phenomena of consciousness, but also illegitimately, as = everything revealed to us in science, whether properly described as phenomena or not. Hence one of two unsatisfactory results. Either (1) the very question of Metaphysics is begged, to begin with; or (2) the word Nature covers both "phenomena," and certain other elements necessary to the existence of phenomena, but very different in kind. The confusion of thought thus arising, is obvious and fatal. Green avoids this confusion by refusing to employ "nature" or "natural" for anything beyond phenomena in the accepted scientific sense. This is what he means by saying *(e.g., Proleg.* § 52) "Nature implies something other than itself, as the condition of its being what it is." Something "other," that is, from "nature," as Sensationalism uses the term; not "other" from nature, as Aristotle or Plato would use it. The following quotation from *Proleg.* § 54, explains his choice of the word "spiritual":—"Nature in its reality, or in order to be what it is, implies a principle which is not natural. By calling the principle not natural, we mean that it is neither included among the phenomena which, through its presence to them, form a nature, nor consists in their series, nor is itself determined by any of the relations which it constitutes among them. . . . . We are most safe in calling it spiritual, because . . . . we are warranted in thinking of it as a self-distinguishing consciousness. In calling it supernatural, we run the risk of misleading, and being misled, for we suggest a relation between it and nature of a kind which has really no place except *within* nature, as a relation of phenomenon to phenomenon. We convey the notion that it is above or beyond or before nature, that it is a cause of which nature is the effect, a substance of which the changing modes constitute nature; while, in truth, all the relations so expressed are relations which, indeed, but for the non-natural self-conscious subject, would not exist, but which are not predicable of it." This passage will show, among other things, that in introducing the word "spirit," he is not (as certain critics have said) trying to put us off with "theological mysteries."

CHAPTER II.

THE METHOD OF METAPHYSIC

TAKING his stand upon the scientific axiom that the ultimate evidence for the presence, or action, of anything, lies in results inexplicable without it, Green argues throughout from Effect to Cause.[1] The "effect," or result, investigated in Metaphysics, is "that which exists," and the only "thing which exists" for a man necessarily and certainly to begin with, is that of which he is directly conscious in his individual self. In practical life we assume the existence of much else besides—an objective world, other selves, and so forth—but the only scientific basis we have, strictly speaking, is that of which we are conscious. Hence, "What are the facts of my own individual consciousness?" and "What is the simplest explanation I can give of the origin of these facts?" are the two primary questions of Metaphysics.

This method of investigation Green uses both positively and negatively; that is to say, he employs it directly to obtain all the results achievable from

[1] *Proleg. cf.* § 73.

its legitimate sphere of operation, but refuses to advance one step beyond this sphere. He tries to analyse, by direct introspection, the nature of his own mind. What does this consist of? What operations does it seem to perform? What is the method of these operations? What the material operated upon? These are the questions first asked, followed, naturally, by the further question, What is pre-existently necessary in order that these things can be? and, What is the simplest expression which can be given to it? The *necessity* of a metaphysical, or scientific conception, means that without it we cannot explain some fact of our consciousness, some constituent in what we call our experience.[1] We are entitled to hold as necessarily true whatever is required to explain this experience, and only what is so required. To take less is to give up our birthright, to demand more is to unjustifiably arrogate to ourselves what we have no right to at all. Hence, while asking continually "What" and "How," Green definitely refuses to raise the question "Why." The ultimate explanation of anything, possible to us, can never transcend the "facts as we know them," together with what is logically involved in these facts. One law of nature is explained by reference to, or resolution into, other laws; one part of nature is, or may be, explained in terms of other parts, by

[1] *Proleg. cf.* § 14.

means of its relations to other parts—but nature itself, as a whole, cannot be explained. "The old question, Why God made the world, has never been answered, nor will be. We know not why the world should be; we only know that there it is."[1] *Interpretatio Naturæ* is the very kernel of Green's method, which ruthlessly thrusts aside *anticipationes* in any form. Whatever results upon "the best analysis we can make of our experience" must be loyally accepted; anything not so justified has no claim upon us as intelligent beings.

The final outcome of this method of inquiry is the establishment of the three cardinal points—self, cosmos, God; but before passing on to consider the reasoning by which these three factors are proved necessary to the explanation of our experience, it is important to dwell for a moment upon a matter cognate to this question of "Method," viz., Green's attitude to Evolution.

From the time when men began consciously to distinguish between the growth of anything and its completed state, that is from the time of Aristotle downwards, there has been a tendency to divide into two schools of thought, according to the way in which the relation between "development" and "essential nature" is conceived. In Aristotle the question is raised in the simple form—are we to explain οὐσία by γένεσις, or *vice versa?* In modern

[1] *Proleg.* § 100, *cf.* § 174.

times the question is essentially the same, but deepened in importance by the doctrine of Biological Evolution. Admitting the historical fact of change, of growth, of development, are we to look backward or forward for explanation? Is man a product of these historical processes in time, to be explained simply by reference to them, or are these antecedent stages themselves to be explained as a "progress" towards what he is now, or, rather, towards a final ideal not yet realised, but the nature of which is the key to his historical development in time? In language as clear and emphatic as that of Aristotle,[1] Green asserts the latter doctrine—γένεσις exists only for the sake of οὐσία, not οὐσία for the sake of γένεσις. The history of the world is that of an intelligent progress, not that of a purposeless series of materially-caused changes. The only "explanation" admissible of man must be derived directly from an analysis of what he is now, and no account of his history, which derives him from elements incapable of functions he now is found to be capable of, can be accepted as complete. "If there are reasons for holding that man, in respect of his animal nature, is descended from "mere" animals—animals in whom the functions of life and sense were not organic to the eternal or distinctively human consciousness—this does not affect our conclusion in regard to the consciousness of

[1] *Cf.* Arist. *De Part. An.* 640ᵃ 18.

which, as he now is, man is the subject, a conclusion founded on analysis of what he now is and does."[1]

Green does not deny—he fully admits—that man has biologically a history; but he protests against any explanation, biological or other, which cannot account for the facts, or, worse still, which confuses a function with the organ through which that function realises itself. "To say that man in himself is *in part* an animal, or product of nature, on the ground that the consciousness which distinguishes him is realised through natural processes, is not more true than to say that an animal is in part a machine, because the life which distinguishes it has mechanical structures for its organs. . . . . The constituent elements of an organism can only be truly and adequately conceived as rendered what they are by the end realised through the organism."[2] The "end" in man being that of a self-conscious intelligence, which "mere" animals do not, according to biology, possess, it follows that, "in strict truth, the man who knows, so far from being an animal altogether, is not an animal at all, or even in part." The difference between "change, and the intelligent consciousness or knowledge of change," is "absolute"; and we are thus precluded "from tracing any development of the one into the other, if development implies any identity of principle between the germ

[1] *Proleg.* § 83.   [2] *Ibid.* § 79.

and the developed outcome."[1] ἐστι γὰρ ἐξ ἐντελεχεία ὄντος πάντα τὰ γιγνόμενα.[2]

On the other hand, it must be carefully noted that Green's method is not "Teleological" in any bad sense. The knowledge of that "end," in reference to which evolution must be explained, is derived solely and rigorously from the "analysis of what man now is and does." *Interpretatio*, not *Anticipatio*, is still the keynote. That all knowledge comes from experience[3] is a doctrine Green holds as firmly as any "Empiricist"—that all philosophy, metaphysical or moral, must be based upon the answer to the question, "What is experience?" is the fundamental assumption of all his teaching.

[1] *Proleg.* § 84.
[2] Arist. *De Anim.* iii. 7.
[3] *Cf.* Works, vol. i. p. 376. "The fact that there is a real external world, of which, through feeling, we have a determinate experience, and that in this experience all our knowledge of nature is implicit, is one which no philosophy disputes. The idealist merely asks for a further analysis of a fact which he finds so far from simple."

CHAPTER III.

THE RESULTS OF METAPHYSIC

§ 1. GENERAL STATEMENT

INTEGRATION, as opposed to disintegration, is the striking characteristic of Green's metaphysic. "That which is" is a *whole*, not an *aggregate*; an organic complex of parts, not a mechanical mass. This "whole" is not material, but spiritual—a world of "thought relations." Described in the order of our knowledge, it consists of three main facts—(1) self, (2) cosmos, (3) God.

(1) The self = the individual person—self-conscious, self-reflecting, self-objectifying; in contact with, but distinguishing itself from, the world, which becomes gradually revealed to it.

(2) The cosmos = the objective world—intelligible, spiritual; one organic, inter-related whole, of which each part exists, and exists only, in relation to the other parts; wherein is nothing except the work of the mind; a world of ἰδέαι, not of material things.

THE RESULT OF METAPHYSIC

(3) God = the eternal and universal consciousness, for whom this whole exists, of whom it is the objective manifestation, through whom it has come into being, and of whom we are "modes," owing our very existence as rational beings to our partaking in the "divine nature," which uses the animal organism as its "vehicle." In slightly different language, and arranged in the order[1] of existence, we may say that the Universe consists of God, who is Spirit, Creator, and Sustainer of all that exists; the world, which is His ideas made manifest; ourselves, who are His children, partakers in His nature, and so capable of understanding the world, which is His handiwork; capable also of realising in action

---

[1] It is important not to confuse this order with that of our knowledge, mentioned just above. The case for the whole of Green's philosophy stands or falls with the correctness of his theory of the Self or *Ego*. Hence, the one serious attack upon Green (for which see chap. vii., "Green and his critics") has for its main thesis the supposed unjustifiable and illegitimate use of this conception, Self. It must not be supposed that this "Self" is the keynote, or central principle, of Green's philosophic system as a whole. That lies in his theory of Reality, as a spiritual cosmos, implying and manifesting an Eternal Consciousness (God). To this "Whole" we human individuals are not (as far as we know) necessary. It might do equally well without us. But Green's conception of the Self is the foundation upon which the *establishment and proof* of his whole system rests. The "Self" is the one fact we necessarily start with, the primary fact we have to explain. This Green attempts to do by asking what is logically necessary to the existence of the Self, as its nature reveals itself to us on analysis. Hence *our* order is Self, Cosmos, God; but in order of existence (or from the point of view of omniscience) it would be God, Cosmos, Self.

something of the creative energy of Him who *is* what we may *become*.¹

This doctrine, stated baldly thus, seems a startling result to obtain from an "analysis of the facts of my consciousness"; but it cannot be too strongly emphasised that Green rests his case solely on evidence so obtained. If this doctrine be true, he holds, we can explain man as we find him; without it we cannot. In his own words (spoken more particularly with reference to the relation of the human self to God) "Proof of such a doctrine, in the ordinary sense of the word, from the nature of the case, there cannot be. It is not a truth deducible from other established or conceded truths. It is not a statement of an event or matter of fact, that can be the object of experiment or observation. It represents a conception to which no perceivable or imaginable object can possibly correspond, but one that affords the only means by which, reflecting on our moral and intellectual experience conjointly, taking the world and ourselves into account, we can put the whole thing together, and understand how (not *why*, but *how*) we are and do, what we consciously are and do. Given this conception, and not without it, we can at any rate express that which, it cannot be denied, demands expression— the nature of man's reason and man's will, of human progress and human shortcoming; of the effort after

[1] *Cf. Proleg.* § 187.

good, and the failure to gain it ; of virtue and vice, in their connection and in their distinction, in their essential opposition, and in their no less essential unity."[1]

Before considering the three parts of this doctrine separately, it will be convenient to state, in baldest outline, the chain of reasoning by which it is supported.

(1) Self-reflection shows us that the *simplest* elements—those of sense perception—into which we can analyse our experience are such that they *presuppose* the work of the mind; they are νοητά, spiritual or mental elements, not elements of feeling. They exist, further, not in isolation, separately, but in relation; having, in fact, no reality except what they possess in reference to each other and to the self, which is conscious of them. The very meaning of a "fact of consciousness" involves inter-relation —a multiplicity in unity.

(2) This characteristic of the "content" of knowledge implies that the object of knowledge, as it exists before any given individual mind comes to know it, must be of the same spiritual nature, otherwise it would not be knowable or intelligible—would not be an "object of knowledge" at all. In other words, we are driven to the conception that Reality = not only the self of which I am directly conscious, but also an intelligible universe.

[1] *Proleg.* § 174.

(3) This latter fact, the intelligible universe—seeing that obviously I did not make it, but was born into it—implies in its turn a Creator, who is a Self-conscious Intelligence in the same sense that I am a self-conscious intelligence. In Him the "idea of the human spirit is completely realised," but free from human limitations. He is Eternal, Universal, Omniscient.[1]

These three cardinal features of Green's metaphysical doctrine must now be considered separately.

§ 2. THE SELF

Man has a Self, and is conscious of it. This is the point of departure for all idealist philosophy, the one explicit assumption[2] which Kantism — whether new or old—makes. The primary and fundamental characteristic of man is Self-consciousness, and the question, "What is the Self?" or "What is man in himself?" must refer, in the first instance, to this special characteristic. In an

---

[1] *Proleg.* § 187.

[2] It is sometimes urged that Neo-Kantism, at any rate, assumes something further, viz.: That a "hopeless dualism" (as, *e.g.*, the belief in the ultimate reality of both mind and matter) is self-contradictory and untenable. The charge, even if true, cannot be limited to Neo-Kantians, but in no case is it worth serious refutation, for upon it no scientific or philosophic doctrine has ever been based. It is little more than a pious opinion, which gives encouragement to the inquirer after that "explanation which must exist somewhere," even if out of present reach.

important passage in the *Prolegomena to Ethics*, Green states his position clearly, as follows :—[1]

"The question whether a man himself, or in himself, is a natural or animal being, can only mean whether he is so in respect of that which renders him conscious of himself. There is no sense in asking what anything *in itself* is, if it has no self at all. That which is made what it is wholly by relations to other things, neither being anything but their joint result, nor distinguishing itself from them, has no self to be enquired about. Such is the case with all things in inorganic nature. Of them, at any rate, the saying, *Natur hat weder Kern noch Schale*, is true, without qualification. The distinction between inner and outer, between what they are in themselves and what they are in relation to other things, has no application to them. In an organism, on the other hand, the distinction between its relations and itself does appear. The life of a living body is not, like the motion of a moving body, simply the joint result of its relations to other things. It modifies those relations, and modifies them through a nature not reducible to them, not constituted by their combination. Their bearing on it is different from what it would be if it did not live; and there is so far a meaning in saying that the

[1] *Proleg.* § 80.

organism is something in itself other than what its relations make it—that, while it is related to other things according to mechanical and chemical laws, it has itself a nature which is not mechanical or chemical. There is a significance, accordingly, in the enquiry what this nature in itself is, which there is not in the same enquiry as applied to anything that does not live. But the living body does not, as such, present its nature to itself in consciousness. It does not consciously distinguish itself from its relations. Man, on the other hand, does so distinguish himself, and his doing so is his special distinction. The enquiry, therefore, what he in himself is, must refer, not merely to a character which he has as more, and other, than a joint result of relations to other things—such a character he has as simply living—but to the character which he has as consciously distinguishing himself from all that happens to him." This "character" excludes, at once, all theories which attempt to explain the *Ego* as a series of states of consciousness.

Between change and the consciousness of change, there is an absolute difference. Man's self-consciousness is his *punctum stans* through which he is conscious of becoming, of a personal history, of an order of time, and which, consequently, cannot be identified with a moment, or series of moments, in that order. It is in Aristotle's language ἀμιγής.[1] What then, exactly, is this "Self," and what are its functions?

To answer this question it is necessary to go beyond, not only the negative quality the Self possesses of being distinct from a series of states of consciousness, but also the more positive character it has as a point of reference in knowledge. The Kantian description of the *Ego* as the "unity of apperception"—the logical head-centre, so to speak, to which each successive state of consciousness is referred—leaves it, after all, without any definite quality or content. But we cannot treat it so, as if it were a mere logical necessity. We must examine the Self in its daily operations. We must ask what is meant by such phrases as: I feel—I think—I know. This opens up a lengthy vista of psychological investigation, but fortunately the enquiry is, for Green, much simplified by two facts in the history of philosophy, viz: That, by universal consensus, mental faculties or functions have been classified as "higher" and "lower," and, secondly, that all modern (at least) materialistic or empirical attacks upon idealism, turn upon the assumption that the "higher" (the specially human) faculties are derivable, step by step, through the "lower," from elementary forms of unconscious organic life, and can be explained as developments of these by natural laws—can

[1] *Cf. De An.* iii. 4.

be satisfactorily treated, in fact, as natural results of natural operations. If we take, then, man as he now is, and ask, What are the constituent elements of the "lowest" human faculty he possesses, as such, we gain a great double advantage. We confine the controversy to the analysis of an act which "no one doubts he can perform," and we are in a position to say that whatever is found to be true of this "lowest" function, is *à fortiori* true of the higher.

The act which Green takes as one "which it is not doubted that we perform,"[1] is the act of sense perception. What are the constituents necessarily involved in a simple act of sense presentation? It is very commonly supposed that such an act is merely a change produced in "our sensibility" by some external object. Perceptions are regarded as separate, particular, mental phenomena—a series of states of our consciousness produced by objects which exist quite otherwise than in and for consciousness. But a "change in our consciousness," as a psychical fact, must not be confused with "that which we perceive" as an apprehended fact. It is true that perception is necessarily connected with a sense stimulus — a sensation—that there can be no perception without (in Locke's words) "actual present sensation," and this truth has led to the common confusion of

[1] *Cf. Proleg.* §§ 59-65.

the "exciting cause of sensation and the perceived object; which again leads to an extrusion of the perceived object from the consciousness in which perception consists, and to the view of it as an external something to which perception is related, as an occurrence to its cause."[1] But take, as a concrete illustration, anything ordinarily described as a perceived object — this flower, this dog — what are the constituent elements? Let an accepted representative (Mr. Lewes) of the empirical psychologists answer, "Our perception of an animal, or a flower, is the synthesis of all the sensations we have had of the object in relation to our several senses." This synthesis is that of a self-conscious subject, which distinguishes itself at the moment, both from the feelings of which it is conscious, and from their occurrence, as a fact, at the time. It is not a synthesis of feelings caused by the action of external irritants on the nervous system. It is, of course, necessary to a perception of colour, that there should be "a stimulus of the optic nerve by a particular vibration of ether," but "that vibration is not the object perceived in the perception of the colour." If we try to analyse a perception into "data of feeling," and show how a complex sensation is made up of these data, we are not analysing an "act of perception" at all.

[1] *Proleg.* § 59.

Perception[1] consists in the presentation to itself, by a self-conscious subject, of qualities having certain relations to its sense faculties, as such, and of the occurrences of these relations here and now. Indeed, "a sensation excited by an external irritant is not a perception of the irritant, or (by itself) of anything at all; every object we perceive is a congeries of related facts, of which the simplest component no less than the composite whole, requires, in order to its presentation, the action of a principle of consciousness, not itself subject to conditions of time, upon successive appearance, such action as may hold the appearances together without fusion in an apprehended fact."[2]

A perceived object is an apprehended fact, it is a synthesis of relations in consciousness, and the consciousness is a self-distinguishing consciousness

---

[1] *Cf.* Works, vol. i. p. 443. "The relation which constitutes or determines the event is not an event itself; if there were nothing but events passing in time, there could be no relations. The mere relation of sequence between any events would not be possible if there were no unit, other than the events and not passing with them, through relation to which they are related to each other, and the same is even more plainly true of those more concrete relations from which events derive their real character. That psychical events, then, really are knowable relations, or (more properly) that the reality of every such event lies in a knowable relation, is not in dispute. The point is that they are so only in virtue of something else which cannot be an event, and which no account of events in the way of feeling explains to us, but which alone renders possible the synthesis of one order of events as motion, of another as a nervous system, and the relation of one with the other." [2] *Proleg.* § 64.

THE RESULT OF METAPHYSIC

which keeps distinct the self and the various elements of the "object," though holding all together in the unity of the act of perception.

The nature then of this "lowest" form of human knowledge is that it is a synthesis of relations possible only to, and existing only for, a self-consciousness which cannot be any of the things so synthesised—any one (or sum total) of a series of phenomena *recognised as such*. What is true of perception is true *à fortiori* of conception and other "higher" forms of knowledge. As a fact, no one denies that knowledge proper (ἐπιστήμη) is, as such, "out of time," and consists in an ideal inter-related whole. The mistake of the empiricists consists in trying to develop this mental structure out of data which do not contain, even in germ, the elements confessedly existing in the completed whole. It cannot be too strongly emphasised that human experience consists, not of chemical or physical processes in an animal organism, but of *these processes recognised* as such. This "recognition" cannot arise out of, or be any one of, these processes. It cannot be made up of materials differing in kind from itself. *Ex nihilo nihil fit*, and the lowest form in which strictly human experience is found is already a *consciousness* of change. Instead of our self-consciousness pre-supposing for its explanation some prior phenomena, the truth is that the fact of there being phenomena for us, necessarily involves a pre-existing self-consciousness, or its faculty. It is in this reference that Kant's doctrine of the "synthetic unity of apperception" is so true. Without this spiritual, unifying, relating principle—the self—there is no "experience" at all. Nothing can be known by help of reference to the unknown. To explain, with empirical materialism, human experience by reference to "matter and motion" is a ὕστερον πρότερον. Even if matter and motion have an "existence in themselves,"[3] it is not by such matter and motion that the function of the soul can be explained, but by matter and motion as far as known to us, and these consist solely in relations between the objects of that connected consciousness we call experience. Unrelated sense particulars are for us nothing. Even the current phrase "knowledge is of phenomena" bears witness to the fact, that for us nothing exists but a "cosmos of experience" in consciousness.

If this is so, what produces the strong dislike to idealism? If human knowledge is *knowledge* (and all science makes that assumption), and consists of a world of thought relations, why shrink from the logical, necessary consequence, that reality, the object of knowledge, consists in thought relations—is ideal, not material? The explanation lies in the common and deeply-rooted assumption that the "work of the mind" is something we do arbitrarily

[3] *Proleg.* § 9.

for ourselves, so that, almost instinctively, common sense habitually opposes "the real" to "what is in consciousness." A "mere idea"[1] becomes the conventional expression for that which is unreal. Yet Locke (equally with Green) holds the doctrine that "all we know" is the work of the mind, and that the work of the mind = "relations." The question then as to the truth of Idealism takes the shape, "Is this work of the mind ours in an arbitrary sense, and so necessarily opposed to "the real," or is it objectively unalterable and true of "the real"? This takes us to the second part of Green's doctrine—the spiritual nature of the objective world.

§ 3. THE OBJECTIVE WORLD

In the last section we saw that the various philosophical schools agree with Green in holding that human knowledge is the work of the mind, and that the work of the mind consists solely in "relations." Perception and conception alike consist in the presentation to, or the holding together in, consciousness of a multiplicity in unity, an "ideal" whole of parts; the explanation of any one of which consists in reference to the other parts. The important question thus arises, Does this fact guarantee, or does it destroy, the possibility of knowledge properly so-called? In other words, Is this ideal cosmos of experience objectively real? Is the world as we

[1] *Cf. Proleg.* §§ 20-3.

know it identical (as far as it goes) with the world as it is? Can we get through to "reality," or must we remain for ever unable to pierce the barrier of 'phenomena," of mere appearance.

Green approaches this question indirectly by dealing first with the common view that the two things—the world as we know it, and the world as it is—are not identical, and considering the consequences. As typical, though widely differing, representatives of this view, Green takes two thinkers—Locke, representing "the traditional philosophy of common sense," and Kant, author of the famous doctrine that for us "understanding makes nature." These philosophers, though diametrically opposed in their original respective attitudes towards the theory of knowledge, yet agree in the conclusion that the "work of the mind" does not give us "the real." In both cases Green shows that the separation of "nature" from the work of the mind, not only leads to a hopeless dualism from which even "common sense" revolts, but is itself due to assumptions which, strictly speaking, beg the very question in dispute.

Let us take them in order :—

(1) *Locke.* No one is more emphatic than Locke in opposing what is real to what we "make for ourselves,"[1] the work of nature to the work of the mind. Simple ideas or sensations we certainly do

[1] *Proleg.* § 20.

not "make for ourselves." They therefore, and the matter supposed to cause them, are, according to Locke, real. But relations are neither simple ideas, nor their material archetypes. They therefore, as Locke explicitly holds, fall under the head of the work of the mind, which is opposed to the real. But if we take him at his word, and exclude from what we have considered real all qualities constituted by relation, we find that none are left. Without relation, any simple idea would be undistinguished from other simple ideas, undetermined by its surrounding in the cosmos of experience. It would thus be unqualified itself, and consequently could afford no qualification of the material archetype, which yet, according to Locke, we only know through it, or, if otherwise, as the subject of those "primary qualities" which demonstrably consist in relations. In short, the admission of the antithesis between the real and the work of the mind, and the admission that relation is the work of the mind, put together, involve the conclusion that nothing is real of which anything can be said.

This is not a conclusion which either "common sense" on the one side, or Neo-Kantism on the other, is content to accept. Yet there certainly is something in this antithesis between the real and the work of the mind which has led us to this strange result. The solution—if there is one—must lie in the discovery of some unconscious assumption

Locke's teaching makes as to the nature of the "real" and the "work of the mind" respectively. The real = "simple ideas," of which "we cannot *make* one to ourselves." They "force themselves upon us, whether we will or no." The "work of the mind," on the other hand, is arbitrary. A man has but to think, and he can make ideas of relation for himself as he pleases. Waiving, for argument's sake, the question whether this latter feat be possible or not, two things are at once obvious:—First, that upon this supposed "arbitrary" nature of the work of the mind Locke's whole theory rests; secondly, that of that kind of work of the mind called exact science the assumption is actually untrue. The relation, *e.g.* between the angles of a triangle and two right angles no one can think equal or unequal, "as he pleases"; and this fact brings out Locke's error, viz., the confusion of the work of the mind, as such, with that work as assumed to be arbitrary and changeable. If we take the work of the mind to consist of a single unalterable system of relations, which we can of our caprice neither make nor unmake, the supposed antithesis disappears; and we get an "ideal" world, which possesses at least the essential characteristic of "the real," that of unalterableness; and at the same time justifies that imperative demand of common sense, which opposes the real to the work of the mind in the sense of *anticipationes naturae,* arbitrary imagination. Man

THE RESULT OF METAPHYSIC

can "think as he pleases" only within certain limits. Beyond these limits he gets a "real," which assuredly "forces itself upon him whether he will or no"; but this "real" is spiritual, not material; it is revealed to us in exact science, where the antithesis between the work of the mind and the real entirely disappears.

It is important, however, not to go too far in this direction. The considerations as yet adduced do not justify idealism, or even render it probable. They establish just three points. (i.) That to argue that knowledge cannot be of the "real" (*i.e.*, in other words, knowledge is impossible), because it consists of the work of the mind, is a *petitio principii*; (ii.) That error can be accounted for simply as = holding an object to be related as it is not in fact related; (iii.) That the essential characteristic of "the real," viz., unalterableness, is not inconsistent with that real being "ideal"—an unalterable system of relations.

(2) Kant believing also that "all we know" is the work of the mind, thinks of this "work" as very far indeed from something changeable or arbitrary. It is, on the contrary, "universal and necessary," and that, not because our knowledge is composed of "simple ideas given" to us, but because it is a synthetic mental structure, due to laws of our mind, by which the known world is held together, unified, and built up into a complex whole. Locke represents

man as passive in knowledge, and successful only so long as passive. His "activity" leads him only to fictitious and arbitrary creations. Kant, on the other hand, saw clearly that in order to constitute a world of experience, there is necessary a single active self-conscious principle. This "Self" is the "condition under which alone phenomena, *i.e.* appearances to consciousness, can be related to each other in a single universe. This is the irrefragable truth in the proposition that the 'understanding makes nature.'"[1] But this "world of experience," he maintained, was subjective only—a world of phenomena as opposed to "things in themselves"; consequently, no conclusions we arrive at in regard to the former have any application to the latter, although the latter are in some unknown way the "cause" of the former. This doctrine brings us at once to a deadlock. It is, in its result, as fatal to the possibility of knowledge as Locke's sensationalism is, though it arrives at that result by a very different path. If it be true, it follows that all we can say of nature is, that it is *not* what we have in our consciousness. The two things, our experience and the objective world, are put into a "position towards each other of mere negation and separation, of such a kind that any correspondence between them, any dependence of one upon the other, is impossible."[2] They are two wholly unrelated worlds. Kant's doctrine

[1] *Proleg.* § 38.   [2] *Ibid.* § 39.

makes the very conception of a cosmos a mere delusion. "Man weaves a web of his own, and calls it a universe; but if the principle of this universe is neither one with, nor dependent on, that of things in themselves, there is in truth no universe at all, nor does there seem to be any reason why there should not be any number of such independent creations. We have asserted the unity of the world of our experience only to transfer that world to a larger chaos."

Hence both Locke and Kant, leaving us in a hopeless deadlock, fail to satisfy the craving of the human mind for a philosophy which, while allowing for, and, indeed, explaining error, shall show us the possibility of truth. In both alike the failure is due to the separation of the "work of the mind" from "the real." Suppose we do not separate them? The temptation is great, but the argument that *if* we take the work of the mind to be also objectively true, we thereby escape awkward questions, can hardly justify us in doing so, without some direct evidence in its favour. Is there any such evidence to be found? And, if so, how far will it take us?[1]

Green appeals again to the facts of our consciousness. Among these facts is found a clear and recognised distinction between falsehood and truth. Without going outside the "work of the

[1] *Cf. Proleg.* §§ 20-24.

mind" at all (without opposing any unreal to an imaginary real), we distinguish "mere ideas" from scientific truths. Nothing we have in our mind is an "unrelated particular," but some of the relations are found to be unalterable and unchanging, valid for us at all times, and for all intelligence, and admitting of prophetic demonstration, while others show themselves variable and untrustworthy. Further, these latter are themselves explainable by science, *i.e.* by reference to other "unalterable" relations. The engine-driver may mistake a signal, may think, that is to say, that the object before him is related otherwise than it is really related, but this error is itself a "real" psychical fact, and admits of scientific explanation by reference to a world of unalterable laws, a world of unchangeable thought-relations. The opposition is not between the work of the mind, as unreal, and a supposed real—both works of the mind are equally real—but between a judgment which states the relations of the object to be those which, according to the order of the universe, do determine it, and the judgment which states other relations than these. But this very error has a psychical history and nature, which is scientifically explainable by reference to the laws of the same unalterable set of relations, of which it gave such a false report. The "appearances," which are proverbially delusive, do not constitute what we call knowledge. As science

—optical, physiological, and other—advances, we discover not only *that* the senses are deceptive, but exactly *how* they deceive. We are able to prophesy exactly what shape the "appearance" will take at a given time, and to point out the "reality" underlying the appearance. And this reality justifies itself in further experience. The "ideal" structure which science makes, shows itself to be the "truth of things," not only by its own self-consistency, but by turning out true in experience (ordinarily so-called). But this scientifically revealed reality is as much the work of the mind as any fantastic imagination, or any illusion, is. To limit our mental operations to such flights of fancy, is to make a purely arbitrary assumption, which is scientifically untenable, and logically absurd.

If, then, all our "experience," all our knowledge, consists in "relations," if each step in knowledge consists in coming to see new relations hitherto existing, but not hitherto known by us to exist, if error itself be a psychical fact which is consistent with, and explainable by, reference to such an "ideal" world, if a clear distinction is recognisable between the "work of the mind" which is my own arbitrary production and that which is not, between mere ideas and scientific truth — is it possible to avoid the conclusion that logically follows? Knowledge is knowledge, and scientific truth is truth. Reality is given to us in science, not wholly nor completely (science is not omniscience), but validly, however gradual the process of "coming to know" is; and this "reality" is necessarily a knowable, intelligible, ideal reality—a system of thought-relations, an unalterable spiritual whole—not a changing manifold of unrelated, particular, sensations. The evidence is all in one direction. There is nothing on the other side but the assumption that what is in consciousness *must* be opposed to "the real," an assumption, the only ground for which is the distinction between truth and error, which, as we have just seen, is accountable for without it. If we are honest with ourselves, we must hold a metaphysical doctrine to which the only evidence available—the facts of our consciousness—points, and which is not only not inconsistent with experience, but explains and unifies it.

The universe then, as object of knowledge, is a spiritual cosmos—a single all-inclusive system of relations; intelligible to my reason, though not yet all understood. What is there further implied in this? For we cannot stop here. We need some explanation, some theory, at least, of how this cosmos came to be. It involves, in its very nature as a related whole, some "principle which renders all relations possible, and is itself determined by none of them."[1] These relations, some of which

[1] *Proleg.* § 27.

THE RESULT OF METAPHYSIC

I know, but none of which I created, must be the work of an Intelligence similar to my own (though far transcending it in power and extent), otherwise I could not understand them, even imperfectly. Relations are (confessedly) the work of the mind; the universe consists of a system of relations which I come gradually to recognise, but which are, most assuredly, not the work of my individual mind. They must then be the manifestation of a mind—a self-consciousness—which is eternal (*i.e.* out of time) and omniscient, which knows and does in whole what I know and do in part. If it is not so, if the spiritual cosmos of my experience, my conception of an order of nature, so clearly distinguished as science from illusion, is on one side of different and independent origin from the order itself on the other, and yet identical with it, we shall be forced to the belief in some unaccountable "pre-established harmony."[1] We shall be compelled to invent some *Deus ex machinâ* to put us in worse case than that in which Kant left us. He had only two worlds—things as they appear to us, and things in themselves—we shall have three (1) illusion, "mere ideas," the result of our arbitrary imagination, (2) an "ideal" world of objective scientific fact, (3) a world of nature corresponding to and identical in content with (2), but of different and independent origin, *plus* a "pre-established

[1] § 19.

harmony." Is it not simpler to say that my world of scientific truth is (as far as it goes) the real world, and that the self-consciousness which gives it to me is identical in kind with an eternal self-consciousness to which is due both my world and me? *Entia non sunt multiplicanda*, and the simplest explanation of the facts of my consciousness is the one which, *ceteris paribus*, we must adopt. This thought brings us to the third part of Green's metaphysical teaching—the existence and nature of God.

§ 4. GOD

As result of the argument just finished, we find that the cosmos, as we know it, is a single objective system of intelligible relations—the manifestation or handiwork of an Intelligence which is the source alike of both the world I gradually learn to know, and of me. Assuming, then, *that* this single self-existing Consciousness, this divine Person, exists, the questions arise, What is His nature? What His relation to us? Can I, by seeking, get to know Him?

Such questions as these do not offer grounds for hope in the same way that the problems we have hitherto dealt with seem to do. In fact "there is undoubtedly a sense in which these questions, once asked, can only be answered in the negative. The most convinced Theist must admit that God is as unimaginable as He is unperceivable—unimaginable because unperceivable, for that which we imagine (in the proper sense of the term) has the necessary finiteness of that which we perceive; that statements, therefore, which in any strict sense could only be applied to an imaginable finite agent, cannot in any such sense be applied to God. As applied to Him, they must at any rate not be reasoned from as we reason from statements about matters of fact. The practice of treating them as if they were such statements, with the confusions and contradictions to which it inevitably leads, only enhances doubt as to the reality of the divine Spirit; of which we must confess that it is inexpressible in its nature by us, though operative in us through those practical ideas of a possible perfect life, of a being for whom this perfect life is already actual, which, acting upon imagination, yield the language of ordinary religion."[1] It would seem that here our sole legitimate source of knowledge, viz., the facts of our own consciousness, fails us. These have borne true and honest witness to a permanent Self, identical with itself in all our perceivings and knowings; to an intelligible world which we gradually learn to know, and which no one of us, as an individual, created, but found ready to hand. These facts, directly borne witness to, involve further the existence of an Eternal Self-consciousness, for whom the best and simplest name

[1] *Proleg.* § 318.

is God, and whose existence justifies the statement that all which exists is merely "God made manifest." Further than this we can hardly go, except, perhaps, by the use of partial and negative statements. We have a right to argue that He is at least what we are, and is *wholly* what we are *partially*; but the only definite categorical judgment this justifies us in making is, that God is an Intelligence who is consciously an object to Himself. We are sure of this, because only by means of such a consciousness is it that we ourselves possess the complex of relations we call knowledge. Relations imply necessarily a self-consciousness which distinguishes itself from them. On the other hand, negatively "we are further entitled to say that the relations by which, through its action, phenomena are determined are not relations *of* it—not relations by which it is itself determined. They arise out of its presence to phenomena, or the presence of phenomena to it; but the very condition of their thus arising is that the unifying consciousness which constitutes them should not itself be one of the objects so related. The relation of events to each other as in time implies their equal presence to a subject which is not in time. There could be no such thing as time if there were not a self-consciousness which is not in time. As little could there be a relation of objects as outside each other, or in space, if they were not equally related to a subject which they are not

THE RESULT OF METAPHYSIC

outside; a subject of which outsideness to anything is not a possible attribute; which by its synthetic action constitutes that relation, but is not itself determined by it. The same is true of those relations which we are apt to treat as independent entities under the names matter and motion. They are relations existing for a consciousness which they do not so condition as that it should itself either move or be material."[1]

To God the world *is*. We know this because, on our limited scale, the world as far as known also *is*. The relations set forth in, *e.g.*, any exact science are, as such, not in time. They are bits of eternal truth attained to by us, and, once reached, held together by us as *one*—all equally present, not as successive events, but as parts of a whole. But they were not always "equally present," they only gradually became so. To God the world *is*, to us the world *becomes*. In this thought will be found the difference between God and man, and also the relation between man and God. Our consciousness, which holds together successive events as equally present, has itself apparently a history in time. This "apparent state of the case can only be explained by supposing that in the growth of our experience, in the process of our learning to know the world, an animal organism, which has its history in time, gradually becomes the vehicle of an eternally complete

[1] *Proleg.* § 52.

consciousness. What we call our mental history is not a history of this consciousness, which in itself can have no history, but a history of the process by which the animal organism becomes its vehicle. 'Our consciousness' may mean either of two things; either a function of the animal organism, which is being made, gradually and with interruptions, a vehicle of the eternal consciousness; or that eternal consciousness itself, as making the animal organism its vehicle, and subject to certain limitations in so doing, but retaining its essential characteristic as independent of time, as the determinant of becoming, which has not, and does not, itself become. The consciousness which varies from moment to moment, which is in succession, and of which each successive state depends on a series of 'external and internal' events, is consciousness in the former sense. It consists in what may properly be called phenomena; in successive modifications of the animal organism, which would not, it is true, be what they are if they were not media for the realisation of an eternal consciousness, but which are not this consciousness. On the other hand, it is this latter consciousness, as so far realised in, or communicated to, us through modification of the animal organism, that constitutes our knowledge, with the relations characteristic of knowledge, into which time does not enter, which are not in becoming, but are once for all what they are. It is this again that enables us, by incorporation of any sensation to which attention is given into a system of known facts, to extend that system, and by means of fresh perceptions to arrive at further knowledge."[1]

"God manifests himself in us." We are, in our very essential nature, the eternal consciousness, reproduced under limitations of time and animal organism, but retaining the essential characteristic of being out of time as regards our knowledge—as regards that in virtue of which we are men. On the other hand, the world as a whole only *potentially* is, for our consciousness is a process as well as a result. The potential content of our consciousness—knowledge—eternally exists as ideas which we laboriously attain unto. The universe is an inheritance into which we gradually enter; but final possession is not yet.

Why this should be so it is useless and, indeed, unmeaning to ask. We "know not why the world should be; we only know that there it is. In like manner we know not why the eternal subject of that world should reproduce itself, through certain processes of the world, as the spirit of mankind, or as the particular self of this or that man in whom the spirit of mankind operates. We can only say that, upon the best analysis we can make of our experience, it seems that so it does."[2] The facts of human life are only explicable this way.

[1] *Proleg.* § 67. [2] *Ibid.* § 100.

Taking all these facts together, we may sum up as follows:—

"The unification of the manifold in the world implies the presence of the manifold to a mind, for which, and through the action of which, it is a related whole. The unification of the manifold of sense *in our consciousness* of a world implies a certain self-realisation of this mind in us through certain processes of the world which, as explained, only exists through it—in particular through the processes of life and feeling. The wonder in which philosophy is said to begin will not cease when this conclusion is arrived at; but, till it can be shown to have left some essential part of the reality of the case out of sight, and another conclusion can be substituted for it which remedies the defect, this is no reason for rejecting it."[1]

[1] *Proleg.* § 82.

CHAPTER IV.

THE FREEDOM OF MAN

"THROUGHOUT the foregoing discussion . . . . our object, it will be remembered, has been to arrive at some conclusion in regard to the position in which man himself stands to the system of related phenomena called nature—in other words, in regard to the freedom of man; a conclusion on which the question of the possibility of *Ethics*, as other than a branch of physics, depends."[1] In these words Green passes from the Metaphysical to the Ethical portion of his inquiry. It is important to note that the "man himself," hitherto investigated, has been only "man as knowing." Knowledge, or the capacity of knowledge, is very far from exhausting human attributes, as we shall see presently, but to have gone further than this within the limits of the previous investigation would have been a *petitio principii*. We are entitled now, however, to sum up the results reached, and to ask, "Are we justified in going further?"

The outcome of the analysis into "What man

[1] *Proleg.* § 74.

now is and does," is that man, in himself, is Free —and that in two ways.

(1) As not determined by natural forces and relations *in the same way* that anything else in nature (including his own body) is determined. Objects in nature are parts of a complex structure, relation to which constitutes their essence — they can be explained (with sufficient knowledge) by reference to natural forces of which they are the product. Man, *in himself*, cannot be so explained.

(2) Free in the further, more positive, sense of "Free Cause," *i.e.* Man is not only independent (in a certain sense) of the natural world, but is actually operative in that world. Just as he is able, *quâ* knowing, to recognise the handiwork of that Eternal consciousness of which he is a "mode," so is he able to reproduce the creative operative action of that consciousness—both functions being exercised under finite limitations. Man, though made in the image of God, is neither omniscient nor omnipotent.

That this conclusion is the true outcome of the previous investigation Green holds for a twofold reason—negative and positive.

Negatively Green points to the failure of Evolutionists to account for human functions—acknowledged by them as such—from purely "natural" forces. They attempt to define man's intelligence as a product, or development, from a "lower" animal intelligence—instinct, or whatever it may be—which is *not* self-conscious, which *is* determined as a product of equally determined natural agents, and explainable by reference to them. But this is to commit the logical absurdity of defining *ignotum per ignotius*. "We have much surer ground for saying what, in respect of our knowledge, we *are* than for saying what the animals are *not*."[1] If direct introspective analysis of the facts of our own consciousness be considered untrustworthy, *a fortiori* any conclusion in regard to lower forms of intelligence, of which men can only say they are *not* what the human consciousness is, must be even less reliable. We may hold fast the doctrine — it is, perhaps, true — that animal consciousness is identical in kind with the human; but that would merely prove the former not to be "lower" intelligence. Whatever the origin of that consciousness of which we have direct introspective evidence, it must be — even in its lowest forms — already a human consciousness; and let the development be what it may, it cannot effect the analysis of its nature now [2]—an analysis which must be definitely an analysis of what man now is and does.

[1] *Proleg.* § 84.
[2] *Cf. Proleg.* § 83. "If there are reasons for holding that man, in respect of his animal nature, is descended from 'mere' animals—animals in whom the functions of life and sense were not organic to the eternal or distinctively human consciousness—this does not affect our conclusion in regard to the consciousness of which, as he now is, man is the subject, a conclusion founded on analysis of what he now is and does."

Positively we find, as a result of the previous investigations, that man, in himself, has specially and distinctly the power of distinguishing himself from nature. He is "conscious of time, of becoming, of a personal history."[1] Such a consciousness cannot itself be determined by these relations which exist only for it, and through its action. It is most important to notice this characteristic of "freedom" in knowledge. The controversy upon the question of the "free agency" of man is often waged with the implied assumption that "action" (in the ordinary sense of the term) is alone concerned. The Determinist, as such, does not deny the possibility of knowledge—quite the contrary; yet the function of knowing exhibits man as "undetermined" by natural forces in a manner quite as clear as the most unquestioned "voluntary act" could so exhibit him. A reflex movement of a muscle may be explainable as a product of assignable forces, but that conscious analysis and recognition of what is before him, on the part of an intelligent being, which constitutes an act of knowledge, contains elements which cannot be so explained. "Our action in knowledge—the action by which we connect successive phenomena in the unity of a related whole—is an action as absolutely from itself, as little to be accounted for by the phenomena which through it become an

[1] *Proleg.* § 81.

intelligent experience, or by anything alien to itself, as is that which we have found to be implied in the existence of the universal order."[1] In respect of knowledge alone—apart from any other capacity, real or supposed—man "exerts a free activity—an activity which is not in time, not a link in the chain of natural becoming, which has no antecedents other than itself, but is self-originated."[2]

We see now a little more clearly what is meant by calling man a "free cause." Cause because he is operative in this world, but free because not operative as a link in a chain of cause and effect in the ordinary sense of the term. By cause and effect is understood "the relation of a given event, either to another event invariably antecedent to it, and upon which it is invariably sequent, or to an assemblage of conditions which together constitute the event into which it may be analysed. Such a cause is not a 'free' cause."[3] It is determined in its turn by other events, whereas man can act "absolutely from himself." He is therefore "free" in the sense that his activity cannot be explained except by reference to itself. It is self-originated. We understand it only through our own exercise of it.

On the other hand, this "freedom" must not be exaggerated. It is equally true of man that he is

[1] *Proleg.* § 77.   [2] *Ibid.* § 82.   [3] *Ibid.* § 75.

empirically conditioned. Not true, of course, of man in himself, *i.e.* of what man peculiarly and distinctly is, but true of the animal organism which is the necessary channel through which his conscious activity works. This truth brings up a difficulty. "Surely," it may be urged, "these empirically-conditioned functions and processes are as much essential to man, as much part of him, as his *e.g.* knowledge is. Your philosophy leaves him still in doubt to deem himself a God or beast, or at best tells him he is partly free, partly determined."[1]

The answer to this objection is teleological—"the constituent elements of an organism can only be truly and adequately conceived as rendered what they are by the end realised through the organism."[2] The processes which are organic to consciousness cease, just because so organic, to be "natural" in the same sense they would be natural if not organic to this consciousness. In a living animal we find mechanical structures and arrangements as organs for the life it displays, but we do not argue that an animal is "partly" a machine because of these mechanical structures. Nor do we regard the latter in the same way that we should if they were not organic to animal life. It may be convenient—for certain purposes it is of great help—to consider abstractly the mechanical structure of the animal by itself as such; equally so the organic processes

[1] *Cf. Proleg.* § 78.   [2] *Ibid.* § 79.

THE FREEDOM OF MAN

of man, but to call the animal partly a machine is not more misleading than to call man partly an animal—animal, *i.e.* in "respect of the processes of physical change through which an intelligent consciousness is realised in him. In strict truth the man who knows, so far from being an animal altogether is not an animal at all, or even in part."[1] His very essential nature consists in the self-consciousness which distinguishes itself from what is around him. Biological evolution, in respect to man's physical nature, may be true, but the absolute difference between change and the intelligent consciousness or knowledge of change makes it impossible that the latter should have developed out of the former; and if—as, until recently at least, science taught—there is not this kind of consciousness in brutes, there can be no growth of our mind from such a mind as theirs. This negation is, however, purely hypothetical—the animal mind may be yet found to be identical in kind with ours. If so, this will raise the brute, not degrade the man.

[1] *Proleg.* § 79.

CHAPTER V

MORAL PHILOSOPHY

§ 1. THE METHOD OF ETHICS

THE preliminary inquiry into man and his relation to nature is finished. It has given us the "proper foundation," without which a science of Ethics is in vain. It remains to build upon this foundation a theory of the individual personal life, not merely as existent, but as *living*—to discover, if we can, what normal life for man is. But at the outset a striking difference presents itself in the subject-matter of the inquiry. If we use the word "is" of the moral world at all, we cannot use it in the same sense as when predicating of the metaphysical world. Hitherto we have been investigating what is actually existing—now, as a matter of fact; but the moral world, though it may picture man as he is when normal, does not, strictly speaking, represent him as he is now, but as he ought to be. The subject-matter of Ethics is not what *is*, but what *should be*. The world of practice is not *given* to man, but made by him for himself. Yet the difference, great as it is, consists solely of a difference in subject-matter, not in faculty. The same Reason, which, working by the method of self-reflexion, gives us the metaphysical results hitherto arrived at, is the source of the moral law which guides our conduct in the world Reason has revealed to us. In a deeper and more practical sense we may say the "World is one"; for the law of our being, by acting in accordance with which we live our true life, is merely the truth of our nature—the statement of the relations in which the individual stands to the spiritual whole, of which he is a part, and to that Eternal Consciousness, of which he is a reproduction. To hold otherwise, to look for a separate moral faculty, would be (apart from the obvious *petitio principii*) indeed to transfer the "unity of the cosmos to a larger chaos"[1]—to deny Him in whom we have our being. "God is not wisely trusted when declared unintelligible. God is for ever Reason: and His communication, His revelation, is reason; not, however, abstract reason, but reason as taking a body from, and giving life to, the whole system of experience which makes the history of man. The revelation, therefore, is not made in a day, or a generation, or a century. The divine mind touches, modifies, becomes the mind of man, through a process of which mere intellectual conception is only the beginning, but of which the gradual complement is an unexhausted

[1] *Cf. Proleg.* § 39.

series of spiritual discipline through all the agencies of social life."[1] The Ethical inquiry is not opposed to the Metaphysical, it is merely carrying out into the special relations of social life that investigation into man's nature which Metaphysics began.

There can be no doubt, according to this teaching, in answering the question, "What is the proper method of Ethics?" Green rejects as unnecessary, untrue, gratuitous, the assumption of a "Separate Moral Faculty" in any shape. On the other hand, while seeing fully the value of "experience" in correcting and filling up the imperfect conceptions of moral duties resulting from man's finite and incomplete knowledge, he refuses to rest satisfied with any merely "Empirical" association of desirable effects with certain lines of conduct. Still less is he content to take feelings of pleasure as the criterion and end of human activity. Life itself is the end, life itself the test, of action. What is true or normal life?—the one question of Ethics—can only be discovered, as well as guaranteed, by self-reflexion gradually revealing to us human capacity, human function, and, consequently, human responsibility. This method, of which Plato is the earliest exponent, is called technically the "Metaphysical" method of Ethics, because it bases the answer to the Ethical question, "What ought man to do?" solely upon the results arrived at in the previous

[1] Works, vol. iii. p. 239.

Metaphysical inquiry, "What is man?" It is distinguished from other "Methods" in three distinct references, viz., Faculty, Operation, Content, which it will be convenient to treat separately.

(1) *Faculty.* The Moral Faculty is that same Reason which has guided us hitherto, and is the source of all our knowledge—Ethical and other. Its origin is the Eternal Consciousness of which we are reproductions, and by which we are able to conceive ourselves as not only existing in certain relations to the world, but as possessing potentialities for more complete relationship. Owing to it we see not only what we are, but also what we may be. It renders us conscious of wants, of capacities for development beyond a present state into a better; from which again we rise to the conception of a possible "best," in which alone final satisfaction may be found. It is in these conceptions that the key to human effort, *i.e.* the key to the concrete social institutions around us, is to be found. They represent the definite capabilities which, revealed by reason, man has tried to realise. The consciousness of having these capacities has been "the parent of the institutions and usages, of the social judgments and aspirations, through which human life has been so far bettered."[1] Man's true good would be their complete realisation; and the idea of them, which is the preliminary *sine qua non* of any effort to attain

[1] *Proleg.* § 180.

this realisation, is given to us by that same Reason to which we owe all our knowledge of human nature. The individual man's "conscience"[1] (so-called) is only the "reason within him" reflecting upon, and influenced by, that "reason without him" manifest in the structure and controlling sentiment of society. It has no doubt a history, but it is a "history which does not carry us back to anything beyond reason. It is a history of which reason is the beginning and the end."

Reason then being the "Faculty" of Ethics, what exactly is its mode of (2) *Operation?* The answer is "Self-reflexion," the analysis of the facts of our consciousness. No other method is admissible except at the cost of begging the very question at issue. For good or ill we must, with Plato and Aristotle, listen to reason as our best guide—the only guide worthy of trust on the part of beings such as we believe ourselves to be. It operates always in the same way—by analysis of the subject-matter in hand. It "interprets" our nature, it does not "anticipate" it. In emphatic language Green urges that "Self-reflexion is the only possible method of learning what is the inner man or mind that our action expresses . . . Judgments so arrived at must be the point of departure for all enquiry into processes by which our actual moral nature may have been reached."[2] Inquiries into the nature of

[1] *Cf. Proleg.* §§ 216-7.   [2] *Ibid.* § 94.

animal movements, animal processes, etc., etc., are in themselves of great scientific value, but "whatever the result of such enquiries, it can only be through a confusion that we allow them to affect our conclusions in regard to the actuality of our conscious life." In fact, "our knowledge of what that life is may not seldom entitle us to reject speculation as to a process[1] by which it has come about, on the ground that such a product as can be legitimately traced from the process is not the inner life which we know. But no inference from such supposed processes can entitle us to decide that this life is not that which a sufficiently comprehensive view of the evidence afforded by itself would authorise us in taking it to be; since the acceptance of this evidence as the given reality is the presupposition of any enquiry into a process by which the given reality has come to be."

The "Faculty" of Moral Science, as of all other science, is Reason; the method of operation is, as always, analysis of the "given reality"; the "reality" given us in ethical investigations is the Self. Not any abstract self, any mere logical point of reference, but the concrete actual self, clothed with the wealth of relations—family and social—in which it lives and moves. This brings us to the (3) *Content* of Ethics. The "content" of Ethics, *i.e.* the formulated results of the Science, consists of a body of Moral

[1] *Cf.* Remarks on the relation of οὐσία to γένεσις, *supra*, pages 16–18.

Judgments. These judgments are statements of what we "ought to do" under definite conditions, or in other words, of what man actually does when acting normally. At any given moment an agent, possessed of definite capacities, is in relation to an environment exhibiting certain definite qualities. The relation so established must be actualised. Reason reveals these capacities and relations by analysis of the self and its surroundings, and so deduces the true ἔργον, or function of this or that kind of man (not man in the abstract) under the given conditions. In this way the content of Ethics—the things which it is right for us to do—varies from generation to generation, owing to the same cause from which moral judgments derive in the first place their origin; viz., reflexion upon the self and the surroundings. This reflexion gives us definite conceptions of a "good," as yet potential, to be made actual. What shape this "good" has taken in the minds of men can be seen objectively in the social and political institutions received from our predecessors. But this very power of self-objectivisation carries with it the capacity to see imperfections and incompleteness in these conceptions of the good for man. Hence the evidence reveals not only a "good," but also a "better," which itself forms a step to a possible "best," more or less dimly visible, and stimulates our effort to realise more completely the ideal which we feel to be our true self. History makes manifest the progress in the past, and helps to guarantee, as well as correct, the analysis of the actually present. If we are honest with ourselves we cannot doubt what the previous conceptions of human good have been—they are manifest in social institutions and accepted Moral laws—nor can we fail to see some better conception in which the self will find satisfaction, and which clearly marks out the path it is our duty to travel. These conceptions, formulated into Moral Judgments, are the "content" of the Science of Ethics.

§ 2. THE POSSIBILITY OF ETHICS

We have been anticipating a little, but unavoidably. In sketching, however slightly, a "method" of Ethics it is impossible to avoid foreshadowing results which, for the moment, seem to be taken for granted, but which do not carry their justification on the surface. The language used in the preceding section implies (1) That man is qualified by attributes rendering an Ethical science possible which is not a science of him in the same sense that *e.g.* Physiology is, (2) That he looks forward to a Moral Ideal to be attained unto by conscious effort on his own part, not backward to a series of natural changes through which he has come to be what he is, (3) That his history is a history of progress of which the explanation lies in this ideal, as the end toward which he is travelling.

These implications require justification by the Method of Self-reflexion alone open to us. No other evidence is admissible. Only if the "analysis of the facts of our consciousness" reveals attributes or capacities logically involving these results are we justified in holding to them. First, as to the "Possibility" of Ethics.

This Possibility rests upon three facts of human life, which may be stated baldly, as follows :—[1]

(1) In all conduct to which moral predicates are applicable, a man is an object to himself.

(2) Such conduct—equally, whether virtuous or vicious—expresses a motive consisting in an idea of personal good, which the man seeks to realise by action.

(3) The presentation of such an idea is not explicable by any series of events in time, but implies the action of an eternal consciousness, which makes the processes of animal life organic to a particular reproduction of itself in man.

We have seen already, in the Metaphysical portion of our inquiry, that the essential characteristic of man is that he is a "Self," and is conscious of it. Conscious, also, of his distinction from, and yet relation to, the world, of which he is a part, and that Eternal Consciousness in whom that world and he have their being. But this very consciousness brings out clearly that, though man

[1] *Proleg.* § 115.

is φύσει a normal part of a normal whole, yet, at any given moment, he may be actually not so. Something is needed that he may *become* what he recognises that (when his true self) he *is*. The world of experience differentiates from the world of practice. In the former, the objects revealed "carry their reality with them";[1] in the latter, the reality has still to be given to that which, as yet, exists only in idea. The objects of the moral world exist in consciousness prior to their existence in reality in the ordinary sense of the term. The explanation of this fact is that man is consciously an object to himself, and actuated, as a consequence, not by *wants*, but by *motives*, *i.e.* by an idea of an end which he presents to himself and strives and tends to realise. This "end," again, is always a "personal good" in some form. The animals have "wants," but (as far as we know) they do not consciously present these wants to a Self as an end in "which that Self would find satisfaction," any more than in knowledge they are (apparently) aware of the facts of their consciousness *as such*. Man always is actuated by this conception of himself as satisfied. In other words, human actions are determined by motives.

In this phrase, "determined by motives," Green expresses his divergence from both Determinism, on the one side, and Voluntarianism, as popularly

[1] *Proleg.* § 86.

represented, on the other. The form of expression is directed emphatically against the "arbitrariness" in the popular conception of the Freedom of the Will, but in its meaning it vindicates human responsibility in the fullest sense of the term. Verbally it is identical with Determinist doctrine as ordinarily formulated, and Green does not shrink from the admission that, "rightly understood," the statement "action is always produced by the strongest motive" is true. The meaning attached to the word motive is the important point —if one sense of the word be taken, action becomes impossible; if another, man is left a free and responsible agent. In any case, however, Green agrees with the Determinists in rejecting the popular conception of Free will. According to this latter conception, man, before any given act, is affected by various desires, or motives, often conflicting, not one of which determines his act, but between which he makes a choice. No reason is given why he chooses this, and not that. He is free in the sense of being arbitrary—his choice is not itself determined by a motive, or by anything else; and this arbitrary, unintelligible choice, is called an "act of will."

Against this conception of an "act of will," Green protests that it is void and unmeaning. It is true that before an act a man may often be legitimately described as "torn by conflicting desires," or appealed to by various motives; but so long as this state lasts he cannot, strictly speaking, be said to "desire," or to have any "motive" at all. A motive is something with which he identifies himself, some object in the realisation of which he believes the self will be satisfied, and towards the attainment of which the whole man himself is directed. Unless there is some such definite object, there is no "act of will" at all. But this consideration brings out also the ambiguity and the unsatisfactoriness of the Determinist position, according to which "the motive which, possibly after a period of conflict with other motives, ultimately proves the strongest, necessarily determines the act." This view ignores the fact that the motive cannot, *ex vi termini*, be identified with one of the desires or aversions which conflict "*before* the man has made up his mind." If so, the man would act, or rather be moved, in several different directions at one and the same time, which is absurd. The actual "desire" which he seeks to gratify may be found ultimately to be one of these preliminary claimants for his notice, but *as such* they are not his desire, nor the motive for his act. As well say that the candidates for a Professorship are as such the elected Professor. The motive is that object with which the man identifies himself as his good or satisfaction, and not until then is it a motive. This motive does necessarily determine the act. The act may be wrong, the object sought one in which true self-satisfaction cannot be found; but this is an error of judgment, not the triumph of some "strongest desire" in the sense of something "outside" a man drawing him on "in spite of himself." There is no parity—nothing, strictly speaking, in common, between these impulses which have been previously soliciting the Will, and that object with which he identifies his self-satisfaction. It is because the phrase "strongest motive"[1] seems to imply this parity that (in spite of a certain truth[2] it contains) it is so misleading. In fact, it "may very well happen that the desire which *affects* a man most strongly is one which he decides on resisting. In spite of its strength, he cannot make *its* object *his* object, the object with which he seeks to satisfy himself."[3] The desires (so-called) with which a man does not identify his self-satisfaction, and the desire in the satisfaction of which he sees his good, will be found to differ emphatically from each other; and it is only the latter which can be properly described as the "motive determining the act."

[1] *Proleg.* § 105.
[2] *Cf.* § 97. "We admit at once that, if he is not free or self-determined in his motive, he is not free at all. To a will free in the sense of unmotived we can attach no meaning whatever. . . . We know of no other expression of Will but a motive in the sense above explained, or, as it may be called to avoid ambiguity, a strongest motive. Such a motive is the Will in act. The question as to the freedom of the Will we take to be a question as to the origin of such a strongest motive."
[3] *Proleg.* § 105.

Herein lies man's freedom, man's responsibility. He is free, not as undetermined by motive, but in the fact that the motive lies in the man himself. He makes it, and is responsible for it. The "Possibility of Ethics" does not arise from a supposed power of "Unmotived Willing," but from the fact that motives cannot legitimately be regarded as natural phenomena, in the same sense in which processes of vegetable growth or conditions of animal wants are such. These phenomena are out of our power. They are natural events following natural sequences; but the consciousness of a wanted object differs absolutely in kind from such a want. It involves a process of self-conscious presentation to which the animal (as far as we know) is a stranger; but which in any case cannot be accounted for by a mere preponderance in strength on the part of one among other conflicting impulses. They come and go; but the self to which they are all referred as they arise is a permanent fact, and it is this self-reference which constitutes essentially a desire or motive in the proper sense. Desire "implies on the part of the desiring subject (a) a distinction of itself at once from its desire and from the real world; (b) a consciousness that the conditions of the real world are at present not in harmony with it, the subject of the desire; (c) an effort, however undeveloped or misdirected, so to adjust the conditions of the real world as to procure satisfaction of the desire."[1] It may be true that a "want" is a necessary presupposition of a "motive," so is possibly sensation to a perception;[2] but just as a perception consists not of the sensation, but of a sensation definitely recognised as such, so in the Ethical sphere a motive is not the animal want, but a want, or rather wanted object, definitely recognised as that in the attainment of which the self will find its true good or satisfaction. An element may be a necessary constituent of something without being in any intelligible sense that thing itself. Take for example the life of a living body. To this living body certain mechanical or chemical processes are necessary; but unless a man is prepared to maintain that these processes of themselves constitute the life, he cannot legitimately argue that life is a chemical or mechanical process. Analogously a "moral action, *i.e.* an action from motives, is not a natural event, because natural want is necessary to it, unless the self-consciousness in and through which a motive arises out of the want is itself a natural event, or series of events, or a relation between events."[3] None of these three alternatives can seriously be held to constitute the "Self" of which we are directly conscious—of that self "which throughout the successive stages, the abatements and revivals, of a want presents the single idea of the self-satisfaction to be attained in its filling; which unites successive

[1] *Proleg.* § 132.   [2] *Cf. supra*, p. 28.   [3] *Proleg.* § 89.

wants in the idea of a general need for which provision is to be made, and holds together the successive wants and fillings as the connected but distinct incidents of an inner life, as an experience of happiness or the reverse."[1] But to reject these alternatives is to admit that that which constitutes the very essence of a "motive" is not to be explained as a determination by antecedent events, or by any other conditions of which it is not itself the source.

Human[2] action may thus be explained somewhat as follows: A want—animal or other, conditioned by antecedent natural events—arises and is presented to the self in consciousness *as such;* it is recognised as something in which self-satisfaction will be found, a means by which that self would become its true self (which at the moment *eo ipso* it is not); by this recognition the want is transformed into a motive, *i.e.* an end in which the self perceives its good, and which it tries to realise. Human character is built up of the self thus

---

[1] *Proleg.* § 90.

[2] *Cf.* Works, ii. p. 337. "The condition of a moral life is the possession of Will and Reason. Will is the capacity in a man of being determined to action by the idea of a possible satisfaction of himself. An act of Will is an action so determined. A state of Will is the capacity as determined by the particular objects in which the man seeks self-satisfaction; and it becomes a character in so far as the self-satisfaction is habitually sought in objects of a particular kind. Practical reason is the capacity in a man of conceiving the perfection of his nature as an object to be attained by action. All moral ideas have their origin in reason, *i.e.* in the idea of a possible self-perfection to be attained by the moral agent."

successively determined by the consciousness of these ends, and the desire to realise them; the identification of the Self with a motive constitutes an act of Will, and the fact that all human action, with consequent human character, is due to this Self-determination, constitutes Freedom.

The Will is free because the man is free. The Will is simply the man. It is no separate Faculty co-ordinate with other faculties. If it were, the man would be as much determined as if his movements were regulated by external necessity. He would be a slave to one of his own attributes. Nor is it abstract or blind force. An act of Will is illumined by the conception of a definite good, which comes clothed with the warmth of feeling, and is legitimately called an "object of desire." This object is so constituted by the man himself, and the movement towards it is a Self-determination. "Will, then, is equally and indistinguishably desire and thought — not, however, *mere* desire or *mere* thought, if by that is meant desire or thought as they might exist in a being that was not self-distinguishing and self-seeking, or as they may occur to a man independently of any action of himself; but desire and thought as they are involved in the direction of a self-distinguishing and self-seeking subject to the realisation of an idea. If so, it must be a mistake to regard the Will as a faculty which a man possesses along with other faculties — those of desire, emotion, thought, etc.— and which has the singular privilege of acting independently of other faculties, so that, given a man's character as it, at any time, results from the direction taken by those other faculties, the Will remains something apart, which may issue in action different from that prompted by the character. The Will is simply the man. Any act of Will is the expression of the man as he, at the time, is. The motive issuing in his act, the object of his Will, the idea which, for the time, he sets himself to realise, are but the same thing in different words. Each is the reflex of what, for the time, as at once feeling, desiring, and thinking, the man is. In willing he carries with him, so to speak, his whole self to the realisation of the given idea. All the time that he so wills, he may feel the pangs of conscience, or (on the other hand) the annoyance, the sacrifice, implied in acting conscientiously. He may think that he is doing wrong, or that it is doubtful whether, after all, there is really an objection to his acting as he has resolved to do. He may desire some-one's good opinion which he is throwing away, or some pleasure which he is sacrificing. But for all that, it is only the feeling, thought, and desire, represented by the act of Will, that the man recognises as, for the time, himself. The feeling, thought, and desire, with which the act conflicts, are influences that he is aware of, influences to which he is susceptible, but they are not *he*."[1]

§ 3. THE MORAL IDEAL

The spring of action, we have seen, is (in Aristotelian phraseology) a "final," not an "efficient" cause. Man is not pushed on by blind force from behind, he strives to realise an end which lies before him. His action may be "determined by motive," but this "motive" is an idea, actual as yet only in the mind of a self-conscious personality, but the realisation of which, in concrete fact, is recognised as a true "good." This interpretation of motive implies definitely that human life has a real "end"—a final "Good" or "Ideal"—which however impossible *practically* of present realisation, exists as a possibility for us, and may be said to be a present reality in the divine mind which constitutes our own true self. For not only is this conception of a final end logically involved in the previous discussion on the nature of motive, but follows necessarily from the metaphysical conclusions upon which our Ethics rests. These conclusions, expressed in terms of the moral life, may be summarised as follows:—

"Through certain *media*, and under certain consequent limitations, but with the constant characteristic of self-consciousness and self-objectification,

[1] *Proleg.* § 153.

the one divine mind gradually reproduces itself in the human soul. In virtue of this principle in him, man has definite capabilities, the realisation of which, since in it alone he can satisfy himself, forms his true good. They are not realized, however, in any life that can be observed, in any life that has been, or is, or (as it would seem) that can be lived by man as we know him; and for this reason we cannot say, with any adequacy, what the capabilities are. Yet, because the essence of man's spiritual endowment is the consciousness of having it, the idea of his having such capabilities, and of a possible better state of himself, consisting in their further realization, is a moving influence in him. It has been the parent of the institutions and usages, of the social judgments and aspirations, through which human life has been so far bettered; through which man has so far realised his capabilities, and marked out the path that he must follow in their further realization. As his true good is, or would be, their complete realisation, so his goodness is proportionate to his habitual responsiveness to the idea of there being such a true good, in the various forms of recognised duty and beneficent work in which that idea has so far taken shape among men."[1]

The moral ideal, moral goodness, moral progress, are all here involved, but their exact nature—the concrete clothing to be given to these vague phrases—

[1] *Proleg.* § 180.

is yet very far from manifest. Granting *that* a moral ideal is implied in the facts of human nature we have discovered, granting further (for the moment at least) that this ideal is the conscious purpose of the divine Intelligence, actually to Him[1] present, though not yet realised (or realisable) by us, have we any ground for hoping that this ideal is in any way conceivable by us? Can we look forward to it as a definite goal? Can we use it as a criterion? We are not here concerned with its practicability in the present. The question to ask of such a conception is not, "Will it work?" but, "Is it true?" But even so it might be argued that human thought is just as incapable of conceiving the (or even *a*) "Moral Ideal," as human will is impotent to realise it in concrete life. In one sense this is obviously true—

[1] *Cf. Proleg.* § 187. "When we speak of any subject as in process of development according to some law, we must mean, if we so speak advisedly, that that into which the subject is being developed already exists for some consciousness. We express the same thing by saying that the subject is something, in itself or potentially, which it has not yet in time actually become; and this again implies that in relation to some conscious being, it is eternally that which in some other relation it is in time coming to be. A state of life or consciousness not yet attained by a subject capable of it, *in relation to that subject* we say *actually is not;* but if there were no consciousness for which it existed, there would be no sense in saying that *in possibility it is,* for it would be simply nothing at all. Thus, when we speak of the human spirit being in itself, or in possibility, something which is not yet realised in human experience, we mean that there is a consciousness for, and in which, this something really exists, though, on the other hand, for the consciousness which constitutes human experience it exists only in possibility?"

to understand fully that "one far-off divine event" would be omniscience, not science, but, fortunately for struggling humanity, there are alternatives between omniscience on the one hand, and utter unconsciousness on the other. Man is not yet θέος, but he is more than θηρίον, and even if we ask the question in its most difficult form, viz., what in concrete detail of daily life is the Moral Ideal? we have some clue at least to an answer. We can point to a "better" which is confessedly desirable of realization, even though when actually realized we may be still "worlds removed" from the "best"; and this "better" (again confessedly) is to be found in the development of institutions which are actual parts of the present social life. That for any given individual the will to strive for this better involves a "change of heart" may be true, but no other change is involved. There is no necessity to take refuge in dreams, or to divorce our thoughts from facts of ordinary life. The elements which make for purity, for happiness, for peace, for greater harmony in mutual relations, for a more complete social unity are here amongst us, recognisable and indisputable. We can conceive these elements working more freely than at present; we can picture a life less interfered with by destructive influences —in which what is good is increased, what is evil lessened—without outstepping or ignoring the plain facts of human nature. Such a conception is already a Moral Ideal, but we can surely go further? Without arrogating to ourselves the gift of prophecy, can we not see distinctly certain characteristics or conditions which *must* be fulfilled by an ideal, whatever the actual concrete manifestation of these conditions may be? It would be disloyal to ourselves as rational beings to think otherwise, and however "formal" (in the technical sense) the result of such effort may appear, it need not, if read in the light of the concrete nature we know, be either vague or indefinite.

The Moral Ideal is a state of "well-being." The well-being which, "in a calm hour,"[1] we desire is always an abiding satisfaction of an abiding self. From this simple thought, alone, flow important consequences. It emphasizes at once the great truth—taught us by Plato and Aristotle—that only in the ἔργον of man is true well-being to be found. Our ideal must be emphatically human. It must consist of the development—more or less complete according as our conception is more or less final —of human capacities, human character. No "end" which involves the absorption of men into something else, can be legitimately regarded as "our" end. Pantheism, *e.g.* in any form, refined or crude, may be rejected at once as a contradiction in terms when regarded as a goal for humanity. The true "end" of human progress

[1] *Proleg.* § 234.

must be a state in "the attainment of which persons — agents who are ends to themselves — are not extinguished"[1] but continue to exist. It is true that we are "manifestations of a divine principle"; but "it is clearly of the very essence of the doctrine above advanced, that the divine principle, which we suppose to be realising itself in man, should be supposed to realise itself in persons, as such. But for reflection on our personality, on our consciousness of ourselves as objects to ourselves, we could never dream of there being such a self-realising principle at all, whether as implied in the world or in ourselves. It is only because we are consciously objects to ourselves, that we can conceive a world as an object to a single mind, and thus as a connected whole. It is the irreducibility of this self-objectifying consciousness to anything else, the impossibility of accounting for it as an effect, that compels us to regard it as the presence in us of the mind for which the world exists. To admit, therefore, that the self-realisation of the divine principle can take place otherwise than in a consciousness which is an object to itself, would be in contradiction of the very ground upon which we believe that a divine principle does so realise itself in man. Personality, no doubt, is a term that has often been fought over without any very precise

[1] *Proleg.* § 189.

meaning being attached to it. If we mean anything else by it than the quality in a subject of being consciously an object to itself, we are not justified in saying that it necessarily belongs to God, and to any being in whom God, in any measure, reproduces or realises Himself. But whatever we mean by personality, and whatever difficulties may attach to the notion that a divine principle realises itself . . . in the persons of men, it is certain that we shall only fall into contradictions by substituting for persons, as the subject in which the divine self-realisation takes place, any entity to which self-consciousness cannot intelligibly be ascribed. If it is impossible that the divine self-realisation should be complete in such persons as we are, or can conceive ourselves coming to be, on the other hand, in the absence of self-objectification, which is at least the essential thing in personality, it cannot even be inchoate."[1]

There is a sense in which we may speak of a national spirit, of a development of mankind, of a change in human nature and the like, as distinct from the individual characters or experiences of the actual persons in whom such development has taken place. But we must not be misled by these phrases. A nation may, for certain convenient purposes, be itself personified or regarded as a more permanent factor in the history of the

[1] *Proleg.* § 182.

world, than any given set of individuals in it; but there can be nothing in a nation which is not in, or is not derived from, the individuals actually composing it. A nation, it is true, is never merely an aggregate of individuals; but, on the other hand, it is never anything opposed to, or separate from, the persons who compose it. The "life of the nation" has no real existence, except as the life of the individuals of which it is made up, and however true it may be (it is a most important truth) that in some sense a nation is "greater" than an individual, of "more value" than an individual, and more stimulative of loyal, unselfish devotion, yet ultimately our "moral value" is always relative to persons as such. "Our ultimate standard of worth is an ideal of *personal* worth."

There are great difficulties, doubtless, in this conception. Suppose it argued that the "analysis of the facts of our consciousness," to which we have been so entirely trustful, reveals capacities of the human spirit which are obviously not realisable in persons existing in any society we know, or can possibly conceive, or even is capable of existing, on earth. The very capacity, *e.g.* of self-objectification, seems to be of this kind. It is of its own nature out of time, eternal. Its aspirations, again, seem often such that, under the limitations of human society, they are impossible of realisation under any conditions conceivable by us. To answer fully these difficulties is impossible; but it may be pointed out that, instead of weakening our faith in the continued existence of "persons," they actually strengthen it. To argue that our personal self shows evidence of capacities impossible of realization under any social conditions we know, may well make us shrink from attempting too much detail in our sketch of the "ideal" society, but can only still further justify our conviction that no ideal which absorbs persons into something "other" or "higher" can be our ideal. It might, indeed, be argued (on our side) that these capacities "justify the supposition that the personal life, which historically or on earth is lived under conditions which thwart its development, is continued in a society with which we have no means of communication through the senses, but which shares in and carries further every measure of perfection attained by men under the conditions of life that we know."[1] On the other hand, doubtless, we may "pronounce the problem suggested by the constant spectacle of unfulfilled human promise to be simply insoluble. But meanwhile the negative assurance, at any rate, must remain, that a capacity, which is nothing except as personal, cannot be realised in any impersonal modes of being."[2] It is true that some capacities do pass away—they contribute their share as means to an end beyond themselves, and are no more (*e.g.* if

[1] *Proleg.* § 185.   [2] *Ibid.* § 185.

natural science speaks truly, the particular capacities of myriads of "low" forms of life); but a capacity which consists in a self-conscious personality cannot be supposed to pass away. It is not itself a series, or one of a series, in time; for the series in time exists for it. It partakes of the nature of the eternal; and we may say finally on this point that "great as are the difficulties which beset the idea of human development when applied to the facts of life, we do not escape them, but empty the idea of any real meaning, if we suppose the end of the development to be one in the attainment of which persons—agents who are ends to themselves—are extinguished, or one which is other than a state of self-conscious being, or one in which that reconciliation of the claims of persons, as each at once a means to the good of the other and an end to himself, already partially achieved in the higher forms of human society, is otherwise than completed."[1]

These last words bring out a further characteristic which a Moral Ideal must possess, if in it we are really to find an "abiding satisfaction of an abiding self." The ideal is not only personal, it is also social. Not that these two conceptions are opposed to each other—still less inconsistent with each other. They are different sides of one fact. "Without society, no persons"[2] is as true as that society is made up of persons. The "self," for certain logical

[1] *Proleg.* § 189.   [2] *Ibid.* § 190.

purposes, is rightly regarded as an abstract point of reference; but the moral self, the "me," the self as actually a factor in the life we know, and of which our ideal is the complete fulfilment, is no "abstract or empty self. It is a self already affected in the most primitive forms of human life by manifold interests, among which are interests in other persons. These are not merely interests dependent on other persons for the means to their gratification, but interests in the good of those other persons—interests which cannot be satisfied without the consciousness that those other persons are satisfied. The man cannot contemplate himself as in a better state, or on the way to the best, without contemplating others, not merely as a means to that better state, but as sharing it with him."[1] Society is the very condition of the development of persons, and its special function is to render possible and to further this development. Hence, our Moral Ideal is necessarily an ideal society — a *whole*, not an *aggregate*, made up of parts in normal inter-relation —each part fully conscious of itself, as such, while finding its true well-being in the relations to other parts, these relations being simply the perfect development of the special capacities of the individual members. Neither aspect of this ideal can be left out of sight; the social whole is indeed organic, it has life and growth, but the parts of the organism

[1] *Proleg.* § 199.

are self-conscious individuals. The final good is, on the other hand, perfection of character; but character can only be formed in the discharge of function, in the performance of duties which are neither egoistic nor altruistic in any significant sense, but which form ἐνεργείᾳ, the very true self of each of us. This is the goal towards which the "good will" strives—the criterion which the "reason" of man applies in estimating the worth of any action or institution in the present. All other "values" are relative to it. "The perfection of human character —a perfection of individuals which is also that of society, and of society which is also that of individuals—is for man the only object of absolute or intrinsic value; this perfection consisting in a fulfilment of man's capabilities according to the divine idea or plan of them."[1]

Here again we are forced back upon the *practical* question; viz., what help, *i.e.* what definite guidance do these conceptions give us in correcting our moral judgments, or in enabling us to state definitely "that which it is our duty to do"? The formal character of the Moral Ideal just sketched may be accepted without question, but even if we admit its value as saving us from utter darkness, it remains at the best a "vacant form of light"; and it is not a form we want, but a content, a filling. Are we really any nearer than before to a conception of

[1] *Proleg.* § 247.

what man's better nature definitely and concretely consists in?

The answer to this question will be (probably) affirmative or negative according to the character, or even the temporary mood, of the questioner. The plan of a house on paper is assuredly nothing at all for a man craving immediate shelter, but in certain other references it might be regarded as almost everything. In regard to a theory of Ethics, especially where even the fundamental basis is a matter of controversy, such a "form" as that given above will be a very haven of rest to the tired enquirer. Few men have been more alive than Green to the pressing urgency of practical questions, but he would plead with Aristotle[1] δόξειε δ' ἂν παντὸς εἶναι προαγαγεῖν καὶ διαρθρῶσαι τὰ καλῶς ἔχοντα τῇ περιγραφῇ, καὶ ὁ χρόνος τῶν τοιούτων εὑρετὴς ἢ συνεργὸς ἀγαθὸς εἶναι. Even if we admit the value to be rather negative than positive, it is no small gain to be delivered from moral anarchy—to gain possession of a definite principle which, if it does not issue of itself a practical command at this or that moment, is ever ready as a criterion to which we may refer a suggested line of action. Time is a sure "fellow-worker" in this matter. If we honestly attempt to realize and develop the actual institutions among us

---

[1] "It would seem that, the outline once fairly drawn, any one can carry on the work and fit in the several items which time reveals to us or helps us to find."—*Nic. Eth.* i. 7, § 17, 1098ᵃ 22.

which "make for righteousness," their permanent good, as well as their temporary limitations, become increasingly clear. "Of what ultimate well-being may be, we are unable to say anything, but that it must be the complete fulfilment of our capabilities ... but of particular forms of life and action we can say that they are better, or contribute more to true well-being than others, because in them there is a further fulfilment of man's capabilities, and therefore a nearer approach to the end in which alone he can find satisfaction for himself."[1] We have to our hand a "better," which is the necessary step on the road to the "best," and must be found in the actual concrete life about us. The "Form" of virtue is constant, but the "Content" is ever changing.

We can see this clearly if we compare the Moral Ideal of Plato and Aristotle with modern Christian conceptions of Virtue. We have, admittedly, advanced upon these thinkers, but in what exactly does the advance consist? It might almost be described as a little matter of quantity—a mere difference in the range of persons denoted by the term "neighbour." Much is implied in this difference in "range," but it is easy (in our self-complacency) to exaggerate it, and to forget that, in what constitutes the very essence of Morality, they were not only on a level with us, but, as

[1] *Proleg.* § 239.

far as we can see, were final. The "end" they conceived—a perfected humanity—is adequate; the distinction of true from seeming virtue, as consisting in the "motive," has never been more clearly expressed; their insight into the fundamental nature of morality as "social well-being," to which each, in his respective way, contributes by the performance, for its own sake, of his duty to his neighbour, is complete; but their answer to the question, "Who is my neighbour?" is sadly narrow. The brotherhood of men — the conception of every human being without distinction of birth or caste, as potentially at least a "citizen," was impossible to them. With the extension of the term "fellow-being" has grown an increasing complexity of application, a larger fulness of detail in the several duties, more numerous channels through which courage, or self-control, can be manifested. On the other hand, we have gratefully to acknowledge that, "once for all, they conceived and expressed the conception of a free, or pure, morality, as resting on what we may call a disinterested interest in the good; of the several virtues as so many applications of that interest to the main relations of social life; of the good itself, not as anything external to the capacities virtuously exercised in its pursuit, but as their full realisation. This idea was one which was to govern the growth of all the true and vital moral conviction which has descended to us."[1] The concrete habits and institutions in which these convictions were manifested, were very far from being finally satisfactory; but these shortcomings, though unavoidable in fact, were in no sense essential to the moral conceptions themselves. The latter could not, certainly, bear full fruit while limited to a small aristocracy of freemen in each community; but the extension in application made no alteration in the nature of the principle. On the contrary, the very definiteness of, *e.g.*, the conception citizenship, was its chief value in saving mankind from moral dissolution, when the old, narrow bonds which had linked men so closely were sundered; and if the moral dynamic of the new era was not the "learning of the ancients," but the "Spirit of Christ," yet the institutions and social relations in which that Spirit was to realise itself were the direct heritage of the old teachers. The Greek philosophers had "provided men with a definite and, in principle, true conception of what it is to be good—a conception involving no conditions but such as it belongs to man as man, without distinction of race or caste, or intellectual gifts, to fulfil. When the old barriers of nation and caste were being broken down; when a new society, all-embracing in idea and aspiration, was forming itself on the basis of the common vocation, 'Be

[1] *Proleg.* § 253.

ye perfect, as your Father in heaven is perfect,' there was need of conceptions, at once definite and free from national or ceremonial limitations, as to the modes of virtuous living in which that vocation was to be fulfilled. Without them, the universal society must have remained an idea and aspiration, for there would have been no intellectual medium through which its members could communicate and co-operate with each other in furtherance of the universal object. It was in consequence of Greek philosophy ... that such conceptions were forthcoming. By their means men could arrive at a common understanding of the goodness which, as citizens of the kingdom of God, it was to be their common object to promote in themselves and others. The reciprocal claim of all upon all to be helped in the effort after a perfect life, could thus be rendered into a language intelligible to all who had assimilated the moral culture of the Graeco-Roman world. For them conscious membership of a Society founded on the acknowledgment of this claim, became a definite possibility. And as the possibility was realised, as conscious membership of such a Society became an accomplished spiritual fact, men became aware of manifold relations, unthought of by the philosophers, in which the virtues of courage, temperance, and justice were to be exercised, and from the recognition of which it resulted that, while the principle of these virtues remained as the philosophers had conceived it, the range of action understood to be implied in being thus virtuous, became ... much wider."[1]

It is to this widening of application we owe the problems which constitute our practical moral responsibilities. Final in one sense the Greek thinker is, but in another his teaching forms for us only a point of departure. We have entered into his labours, but we may not rest there. Our task, like his, is to find out in what the ὁμοίωσις θέῳ, which is the true final goal, really consists. Like him, too, we can only express this end in terms of our day and generation. These terms will appear incomplete to our successors; but at least we are bound to ensure, to the best of our ability, that the new generation shall in them find the light of true essential principles to guide them in the better structure it will be their privilege to build.

§ 4. MORAL GOODNESS AND PROGRESS

The Moral Ideal is the perfection of human character, consisting in a fulfilment of man's capabilities according to the divine idea or plan of them. But this "plan," although in one sense it may be regarded as the eternal purpose of God, is yet left to *us* (in another very real sense) to work out for ourselves, and to work out *consciously*. In the

[1] *Proleg.* § 285.

conscious self-direction towards this definite end, Moral Goodness consists. What exactly this end is in detail we cannot know, except in so far as it has been already attained; but of this we may rest assured, that "the supreme condition of any progress toward its attainment is the action in men, under some form or other, of an interest in its attainment as a governing interest or will; and the same interest —not in abstraction from other interests, but as an organising influence upon and among them—must be active in every character which has any share in the perfection spoken of, or makes any approach to it, since this perfection, being that of an agent who is properly an object to himself, cannot lie in any use that is made of him, but only in a use that he makes of himself."[1]

It is not enough—in order to be morally good— that an action should tend to develop a human faculty, or promote a more perfect social relation. Society, however organic it is, or ought to be, is never *merely* an organism. The goodness of an action, still more the goodness of an individual character, does not depend upon objective excellence alone, or even mainly. The ideal society spoken of in the last section is a society of *persons*, and the one thing in it of absolute intrinsic value is personal character. Now character is built up gradually out of acts of will. This is the truth em-

[1] *Proleg.* § 247.

phasised (though unduly limited) in Kant's famous dictum: "Nothing can be conceived in the world, or even out of it, which can be called good without qualification, but a good will." The right thing must be done because it is *right*—ἕνεκα καλοῦ—otherwise it is not a good action in the proper sense of the term.

Hence, at the very root of any system of Ethics lies the distinction between the Good and the Bad Will. In what exactly does this distinction consist?

Not in the mere "form" of willing. That is common, necessarily and obviously, to every act of Will. In all alike "a self-conscious individual directs himself to the realisation of some idea, as to an object in which for the time he seeks self-satisfaction." The difference lies elsewhere—in the end sought, the idea which is being realised in action. "The real nature of any act of Will depends on the particular nature of the object in which the person willing for the time seeks self-satisfaction; and the real nature of any man as the subject of Will—his character—depends on the nature of the objects in which he mainly tends to seek self-satisfaction. Self-satisfaction is the form of every object willed; but the filling of that form, the character of that in which self-satisfaction is sought, ranging from sensual pleasure to the fulfilment of a vocation conceived as given by God, makes the object what it really is. It is on the specific difference of the objects willed under the general form of self-satisfaction that the quality of the will must depend. It is here, therefore, that we must seek for the basis of distinction between goodness and badness of will."[1]

The meaning of the phrase "specific difference of the objects willed," Green defines as "a difference between them in respect of that which is the motive to the person willing them, as distinct from a difference constituted by any effects which the realisation of the objects may bring about, but of which the anticipation does not form the motive."[2] Good will is *intrinsically* different from bad will. In this view of the real nature of an act of will, Green differs equally from Kantian doctrine on the one side, and the teaching of Utilitarianism on the other. According to the latter, the motive of every action is identical, viz., a desire for pleasure (or to escape pain); the difference consequently in objects willed consists solely in the effects produced. These effects are in every way objective and extrinsic. They are actual results in fact, and they do not enter, as such, into the motive, which is always and solely desire for pleasure.[3]

---

[1] *Proleg.* § 154.   [2] *Ibid.* § 156.
[3] *Cf. Mill's Utilitarianism*, ch. 2. "The creed which accepts as the foundation of morals, Utility, or the Greatest Happiness Principle, holds that actions are right in proportion as they tend to promote happiness, wrong as they tend to produce the reverse of happiness. By happiness is intended pleasure, and the absence of pain; by

It is even more important—in view of the epithet Neo-Kantian, so often applied to Green—to note how greatly he differs on this question from Kant. Kant is, as it were, at the other extreme when compared to Mill. With him not only is the will good, by virtue of what it is in itself (as opposed to any extrinsic effort or result), but the "itself" refers to the will in its purely formal character.[1] It is good because of its own goodness, not because of its content, or the end to which it is directed. Such "goodness" is, however, formal or abstract, and it is not in any abstract idea of the moral law, but in a definite application to some concrete actuality of life that the goodness of the good will consists. A good will, in other words, is the "will of the good workman, the good father, the good citizen."[2] Taken

unhappiness, pain, and the privation of pleasure. To give a clear view of the moral standard set up by the theory, much more requires to be said . . . but these supplementary explanations do not affect the theory of life on which this theory of morality is grounded, namely, that pleasure, and freedom from pain, are the only things desirable as ends; and that all desirable things (which are as numerous in the Utilitarian as in any other scheme) are desirable either for the pleasure inherent in themselves, or as means to the promotion of pleasure and the prevention of pain."

[1] *Cf. Kant. Fundamental Princip.* [Abbott's Trans.] "Nothing can possibly be conceived in the world, or even out of it, which can be called good without qualification, except a good will . . . A good will is good not because of what it performs or effects, not by its aptness for the attainment of some proposed end, but simply by virtue of the volition, that is, it is good in itself, and, considered by itself, is to be esteemed much higher than all that can be brought about by. . " etc., etc.   [2] *Proleg.* § 247.

strictly in its apparent meaning, Kant's dictum would result in a "paralysis of the will for all effectual application to great objects of human interest."[1] The good will is *intrinsically* good not because the moral criterion ignores the objective result aimed at, but because the aiming at this result —recognised as subserving a true human interest— itself enters into the motive of the agent. There may be some virtue—even of the highest kind—in a misdirected effort towards a "common good," but in so far as misdirected, it is not in the proper sense a good will. "There may be as genuine self-devotion in the act of the barbarian warrior who gives up his life that his tribe may win a piece of land from its neighbours, as in that of the missionary who dies in carrying the gospel to the heathen. But it is a falsely abstract view of virtue to take no account of the end in pursuit of which the self is devoted. The real value of the virtue rises with the more full and clear conception of the end to which it is directed, as a character, not a good fortune, as a fulfilment of human capabilities from within, not an accession of good things from without, as a function, not a possession. The progress of mankind in respect of the standard and practice of virtue, has lain in such a development of the conception of its end."[2]

[1] *Proleg.* § 247.
[2] *Ibid.* § 246.

To trace this progress in its historical development would be foreign to the present purpose, even if it were possible. Sketched shortly, we might say that Morality—the good will—arises when a man first conceives himself, as in his very nature, a part of some larger whole, and consciously puts before him the satisfaction of the self, so understood, as his object. To provide, *e.g.* for the wants of a family, is not morally good (in the proper sense) so long as it remains instinctive and unreflective, but to work consciously for the well-being of a family, as an object for its own sake, is so. It implies a totally different motive as compared with either unreflecting response to stimulus, or a mere desire for pleasurable gratification. It involves the conception of a *permanent* satisfaction which, moreover, is only obtainable in the satisfaction of others, in a common good. "Here is already a moral and spiritual, as distinct from an animal or merely natural, interest—an interest in an object which only thought constitutes, an interest in bringing about something which *should be*, as distinct from a desire to feel again a pleasure already felt."[1]

The next step is taken when by reflection upon the (family or social) life occupied so far wholly in the effort to satisfy material wants—goods of the body—men begin to realize that their nature has further capabilities, and to conceive the satisfaction

[1] *Proleg.* § 242.

of these as more worthy and important than that of the others. Security from the pressure of animal want remains as before a necessary condition of life, but it is no longer the sole end, or even the main object, for which men work. In its stead some spiritual want arises—it may be merely a sentiment about the honour of the tribe, or the prestige of a local god—which involves necessarily an effort to make the growing members of the tribe persons of *a certain kind*, as opposed to the desire of providing for them means for personal gratification. Gradually these personal qualities cease to be regarded as means to an end, and become themselves an end. Personal character becomes important, and further reflection gradually evolves the conception of morality or goodness as such. "An interest has arisen, over and above that in keeping the members of a family or tribe alive, in rendering them persons of a certain kind; in forming in them certain qualities, not as a means to anything ulterior which the possession of these qualities might bring about, but simply for the sake of that possession; in inducing in them habits of action on account of the intrinsic value of those habits, as forms of activity in which man achieves what he has it in him to achieve, and so far satisfies himself. There has arisen, in short, a conception of good things of the soul, as having a value distinct from, and independent of, the good things of the body, if not as the only things truly good, to which all other goodness is merely relative."[1]

In this way the idea of the "good," though always "formally" the same—the idea of self-satisfaction—continually changes its "filling," by reflective analysis of the modes of life which have arisen among men in the efforts to realise the idea in action. This development in the idea itself is not, of course, always the important *practical* consideration; a good action, at a given moment, may (generally does) consist in doing something which we know to be right, from a pure motive, and this "something which," in its exact detail, may not vary during the course of a long life. Moral progress, again, in the individual, often takes the shape of more adequate discharge of duties in "that station of life," in which he is placed, unaccompanied by any intellectual advance in the conception of these duties themselves. But if moral progress meant nothing but this, mankind would be at a standstill—would, in fact, never have emerged from moral barbarism. Change in the conception of the idea of good itself is a necessary element in moral growth as dealt with, at all events, by the Science of Ethics. Moral development cannot be limited to "merely progress in the discovery and practice of means to an end which throughout remains the same for the subject

[1] *Proleg.* § 243.

of the development. It will imply a progressive determination of the idea of the end itself, as the subject of it, through reflection on that which, under influence of the idea, but without adequate reflection upon it, he has done and has become, comes to be more fully aware of what he has it in him to do and to become."[1]

Thus we get finally the answer to the objection that to define moral goodness as the good will, and the good will as the will for the good, is either tautologous or unmeaning. Even if we waive the "tautology" (the objector argues) as a verbal accident, what meaning can be practically attached to the word good if (1) it is defined as "that end in which the moral agent can really find rest," if (2) by "end" so qualified is meant "the realisation of the moral capability"; and if (3) it is impossible (obviously and admittedly) to know what this ultimate realisation is, or, without that knowledge, what the capability itself is?

To this objection, though it contains a truth, the "answer is that from a moral capability which had not realised itself at all, nothing could indeed be inferred as to the moral good which can only consist in its full realisation; but that the moral capability of man is not in this wholly undeveloped state. To a certain extent it has shown by actual achievement what it has in it to become, and by

[1] *Proleg.* § 241.

reflection on the so far developed activity we can form at least some negative conclusion in regard to its complete realisation. We may convince ourselves that this realisation can only be attained in certain directions of our activity, not in others. We cannot indeed describe any state in which man, having become all that he is capable of becoming—all that, according to the divine plan of the world, he is destined to become — would find rest for his soul. We cannot conceive it under any forms borrowed from our actual experience, for our only experience of activity is of such as implies incompleteness. Of a life of completed development, of activity with the end attained, we can only speak or think in negatives, and thus only can we speak or think of that state of being in which, according to our theory, the ultimate moral good must consist. Yet the conviction that there must be such a state of being, merely negative as is our theoretical apprehension of it, may have supreme influence over conduct, in moving us to that effort after the Better, which, at least as a conscious effort, implies the conviction of there being a Best."[1]

And when the speculative question is raised as to what this Best can be, we find that it has not left itself without witness. The practical struggle after the Better, of which the idea of there being

[1] *Proleg.* § 172.

a Best has been the spring, has taken such effect in the world of man's affairs as makes the way by which the Best is to be more nearly approached, plain enough to him that will see. In the broad result it is not hard to understand how man has bettered himself through institutions and habits which tend to make the welfare of all the welfare of each, and through the arts which make nature, both as used and as contemplated, the friend of man. And just so far as this is plain, we know enough of ultimate moral good to guide our conduct; enough to judge whether the prevailing interests which make our character are, or are not, in the direction which tends further to realise the capabilities of the human spirit.

A final quotation from the *Prolegomena* will sum up the teaching of this and the preceding section. "Our theory has been that the development of morality is founded on the action in man of an idea of true or absolute good, consisting in the full realisation of the capabilities of the human soul. This idea, however, . . . acts in man, to begin with, only as a demand unconscious of the full nature of its object. The demand is, indeed, from the outset quite different from a desire for pleasure. It is at its lowest a demand for some well-being which shall be common to the individual desiring it with others; and only as such does it yield those institutions of the family, the tribe, and the state, which further determine the morality of the individual. The formation of more adequate conceptions of the end to which the demand is directed, we have traced to two influences, separable for purposes of abstract thought, but not in fact; one, the natural development, under favouring conditions, of the institutions, just mentioned, to which the demand gives rise; the other, reflection alike upon these institutions and upon those well-reputed habits of action which have been formed in their maintenance and as their effect. Under these influences there has arisen ... on the one hand, an ever-widening conception of the range of persons between whom the common good is common; on the other, a conception of the nature of the common good itself, consistent with its being the object of a universal society co-extensive with mankind. The good has come to be conceived with increasing clearness; not as anything which one man, or set of men, can gain or enjoy to the exclusion of others, but as a spiritual activity in which all may partake, and in which all must partake if it is to amount to a full realisation of the faculties of the human soul. And the progress of thought in individuals, by which the conception of the good has been thus freed from material limitations, has gone along with a progress in social unification which has made it possible for men practically to conceive a claim of all upon all for freedom and support in the pursuit of a common end. Thus the ideal of virtue which our consciences acknowledge has come to be the devotion of character and life, in whatever channel the idiosyncrasy and circumstances of the individual may determine, to a perfecting of man, which is itself conceived, not as an external end to be attained by goodness, but as consisting in such a life of self-devoted activity on the part of all persons."[1]

The universe, we have seen, is an intelligible whole. Human life, as part of this cosmos, must admit of rational explanation, and explanation of what is imperfectly developed necessarily involves the conception of a progress, actual at present only in the thought of the Eternal Consciousness. But we are partakers of the Divine Nature, and can understand—if we will only be simply true to ourselves—somewhat at least of the meaning of life and the stages of human progress. Little by little with the passing of centuries we can enter more and more into the divine plan of the world. "God is for ever reason; and His communication, His revelation is reason; not, however, abstract reason, but reason as taking a body from, and giving life to, the whole system of experience which makes the history of man. The revelation, therefore, is not made in a day, or a generation, or

[1] *Proleg.* § 286.

a century. The divine mind touches, modifies, becomes the mind of man, through a process of which mere intellectual conception is only the beginning, but of which the gradual complement is an unexhausted series of spiritual discipline through all the agencies of social life."[1]

These agencies of moral well-being and moral growth are here working in our midst "plain enough for him who will see." The one condition of their fulfilment is, on our part, the "will in some form or other to contribute to it." The one hindrance, the one human wickedness, is selfishness, *i.e.* the preference of private pleasure to the common good. Owing to this preference, we often refuse to contribute our proper share to the well-being of the whole, and sometimes take advantage of the shortcomings of human knowledge as an excuse for shutting our eyes to unpleasant truths. But "it is still our sins and nothing else that separate us from God. Philosophy and science, to those who seek not to talk of them, but to know their power, do but render His clearness more clear, and the freedom of His service a more perfect freedom. His witness grows with time. In great books and great examples, in the gathering fulness of spiritual utterance which we trace through the history of literature. in the self-denying love which we have known from the cradle, in the moralising influences of civil life,

[1] *Witness of God*, vol. iii. p. 239.

in the closer fellowship of the Christian society, in the sacramental ordinances which represent that fellowship, in common worship, in the message of the preachers through which, amid diversity of stammering tongues, one spirit still speaks—here God's sunshine is shed abroad without us. If it does not reach within the heart, it is because the heart has a darkness of its own, some unconquered selfishness which prevents its relation to Him being one of sincerity and truth."[1]

[1] *Witness of God*, vol. iii. p. 248.

CHAPTER VI.

POLITICAL PHILOSOPHY

δοκεῖ γὰρ εἶναί τι δίκαιον παντὶ ἀνθρώπῳ πρὸς πάντα τὸν δυνάμενον κοινωνῆσαι νόμου καὶ συνθήκης.

§ 1. THE GROUND OF POLITICAL OBLIGATION

THE Moral Ideal is an ideal of character manifest in acts in which that character issues. Moral Goodness consists in the will to realise in act the ideal given by the Reason. In this lies the key to the meaning and value of civic life, and the answer to the old question, "Why ought I to obey the law?" Political and social life is merely the concrete shape which Moral Ideas take when they are translated into actuality. Through civic institutions alone is it possible for the idea of moral perfection to be realised by human beings. In criticising such institutions, in asking them to justify themselves, we have to consider what permanent moral value they possess; in other words, how far and in what way do they contribute to the possibility of the moral life—to the development of character. The Moral Ideal, which the good will seeks to realise, is gained, as we have seen, by self-reflexion. It consists in the idea of a possible self-perfection to be attained by the moral agent. But this self-perfection cannot be gained in isolation, by renouncing or withdrawing from the "world." It is realisable only in relation to our fellow-creatures in a social community. Hence, the one definite value which the institutions of civil life possess consists in "their operation as giving reality to these capacities of will and reason, and enabling them to be really exercised. In their general effect, apart from particular aberrations, they render it possible for a man to be freely determined by the idea of a possible satisfaction of himself, instead of being driven this way and that by external forces, and thus they give reality to the capacity called will: and they enable him to realise his reason, *i.e.* his idea of self-perfection, by acting as a member of a social organisation in which each contributes to the better being of all the rest. So far as they do in fact thus operate, they are morally justified."[1]

The ground of political obligation—the reason why I have duties which I "ought" to discharge towards others, and conversely "rights" which I claim from or as against others—is thus clear. It lies in the very nature of man. With Aristotle, and exactly in the same sense as Aristotle, Green holds that civic responsibilities are innate or natural. Not, that

[1] *Pol. Oblig.* § 7.

is, that there are "natural rights" existing when a man is born, or prior to the institution of society; but that the relations which are objectively expressed in civic community arise out of, and are necessary for the fulfilment of, a moral capacity, without which a man would not be a man at all. Man is φύσει πολιτικός, and only in social life is he himself. Hence, the analysis of what man essentially *is* does reveal to us a body of rights and duties which in this sense are innate, but only in this sense. "Natural rights," if by that phrase is meant something man possesses prior to or out of society, and which he carries with him unimpaired into the new social sphere, are a contradiction in terms. Rights and duties imply the clear recognition of a common life with a common interest or good. Apart from such life, and the clear consciousness of it on the part of the individuals who make it up, the words are simply unmeaning. Hence, it follows that "no one can have a right except

"(1) As a member of a society;

"(2) Of a society in which some common good is recognised by the members of the society as their own ideal good, as that which should be for each of them."[1]

This recognition carries with it not only moral responsibilities in the ordinary sense—duties which I see I ought to perform to my neighbour—but

[1] *Pol. Oblig.* § 25.

has a further definite political reference. The individual becomes not only a part of a social whole, related to other parts, he finds himself in relation to the whole itself. Society becomes political or civic, the citizen demands that power or opportunity be given him by society to develop himself in the way in which he is best fitted to play his part for the common good; society conversely claims certain powers over the individual, to regulate his life in a more or less definite way which shall be best for the realisation of this common good. These claims and counter-claims have an appropriate moral basis. They "rest on the fact that these powers are necessary to the fulfilment of man's vocation as a moral being, to an effectual self-devotion to the work of developing the perfect character in himself and others."[1] Civic institutions are the test of the moral progress of a society; they form, in a most important respect, the outward expression of its morality, and "political" obligation is of the same nature as that more usually designated "moral."

Considerations such as these give us solid ground for believing that civic obligations are really binding on us; but they do more than that. They hold out a hope that in them we may find a criterion—theoretically valid, and practically applicable—by which to test any given system of legal

[1] *Pol. Oblig.* § 21.

or political obligations. From the time (at least) of Sophocles men have consciously appealed from the laws they are bidden, as citizens, to obey to higher rules even more valid and binding. The "Law of Nature" has been, and is still, regarded as a court of appeal before which human or positive Law may be brought for condemnation or approval. What exactly this Law of Nature is has been the subject of much controversy, but, if what has just been said be correct, there is a great truth in the phrase. Any rule or institution which can be shown as tending to weaken or destroy the true nature of man, to hinder the development of his "natural" capacities, to put obstacles in the realisation of that ideal of character which is his true self, is *eo ipso* condemned. It is obviously of the most fundamental practical importance that there should be some such test, available and generally recognised, otherwise no progress would be possible. No one (whatever school of thought he belong to) could seriously maintain that the body of rights and obligations actually established in any existing nation is all that it "ought" to be. There is always conceivable a better system, even though no definite single modification in the existing code would meet with universal acceptance. Hence arises the important practical question, "Are we entitled to distinguish the rights and obligations which are anywhere actually enforced by law from rights and obligations which really exist, though not enforced?"[1] If so, what is to be our criterion, and in what sense are these (higher or truer) rights valid as against those actually enforced?

The conception of the moral function of the State gives us the answer to these questions. We can point to the definite end which it is the vocation of human society to realise—the Moral Ideal—the normal or perfect development of man as such. We only know this ideal in the sense, and with the limitations, pointed out in the preceding chapters, but that is amply sufficient for practical purposes, for politics is even less exacting in this respect than ethics. In this way we can get the conception of a system of rights and obligations which *should be* maintained by Law, whether it is so or not. To this bar we can call any actually existing system, and demand it should justify itself.

The function, then, of Law and of civic institutions is to help man to realise his idea of self-perfection as a member of a social organisation in which each contributes to the better being of all the rest. In this fact of "nature" lies the true ground of political obligation. We are to act worthily of the vocation wherewith we are called, and the vocation of each one of us is to be an

[1] *Pol. Oblig.* § 8.

integral part of a social whole. Duty calls us to perform our function; rights consist in our claim that others should in like manner fulfil theirs; institutions are the concrete embodiment of the complex inter-relations of the social organism, and life itself is the ultimate justification of each citizen's obligation to support these institutions. It is true that "institutions" are not perfect, and that difficult questions[1] sometimes arise as to the possibility that a citizen's "duty" may be occasionally to destroy rather than to fulfil, but, speaking broadly, we can affirm that, civic institutions being the actual realisation of human capabilities, the ground of obligation in regard to them lies in the very nature of man himself. The phrase, *jus naturae* — Law of Nature — has often been misused, but understood rightly it bears witness to fundamental truth; for

"There's on earth a yet auguster thing,
   Veiled though it be, than Parliament and King";

viz., Humanity itself. Civic responsibilities, as well as moral, or rather *because* they too are moral, must be deduced from the essential nature of man. Their formulation is the answer, more directly and practically than ethical laws ordinarily so-called, to the inquiry "what man is and ought to do." Whatever be the result of the inquiry,

[1] For these questions see §§ 3, 4.

there can be no other, certainly no surer, ground of political obligation than that based upon such analysis.

§ 2. OTHER POLITICAL THEORIES

The phrase "Law of Nature" has thus a real meaning, nor need we shrink even from speaking of "Natural Rights" if we are careful to remember in what sense exactly they are "Natural," and what constitutes them "Rights." They are necessarily implied in the existence of any Society which is conscious of itself as such, and are, primarily, statements or formulations of the inter-relations of the parts of the social whole. Green's use of the word "right" is entirely consistent with accepted present teaching. Professor Holland, *e.g.*, defines a right as "one man's capacity of influencing the acts of another, by means, not of his own strength, but of the opinion or the force of society,"[1] and is at one with Green in declaring that "to talk of law and right, as applied to mankind at a supposed period anterior to society beginning to think and act, is a contradiction in terms."[2] What the professional lawyer, however, brings forward merely as the definition of a fact, is in Green presented along with its philosophical justification.

This positive statement of the nature of a "right," and the consequent ground for political obligation,

---

[1] *Elements of Jurisprud.* ch. vii.   [2] *Ibid.* ch. iii.

is perhaps sufficiently plain, but the importance of a clear conception on this matter is so fundamental, and the confusions of controversy so manifold and so fatal, that we require to dwell somewhat on certain well-known, but erroneous uses of the term if we are to realise fully the true nature of this root-conception of politics. The part played by certain interpretations of it in modern history—more particularly in England, France, and the United States—is amply sufficient to justify a short criticism of the teaching of Spinoza, Hobbes, Locke, and Rousseau, in order that the conception of the true meaning of a "right" may be deepened and enlightened by contrast.

(1) *Spinoza.*

Of the great truth upon which Green insists so strongly; viz., that "natural right," if it be taken in the sense of a "right," existing in a state of nature apart from or prior to Society, is a contradiction in terms, Spinoza seemed quite aware./ With him *jus naturae* = neither more nor less than *potentia naturae*. Unfortunately, by a confusion of thought he still regarded it as *jus*, and held that no other relation between man and man, individual and State, or between different States, is "right" except that of *potentia*. Considerations of the moral life, of a social whole of parts regulated by right reason, must be put on one side as irrelevant. The only things which a State has no "right" to do are those things which, as a matter of fact, tend to lessen its " power." Undue severity, for example, or tyrannous oppression, would tend to cause dissatisfaction and conspiracy on the part of the subject citizens, and so weaken the State.

Does Spinoza's teaching, then, come simply to this, that "Might is Right"?

In so far as he is consistent with himself—yes; but he is not consistent. *Non id omne quod jure fieri dicimus, optime fieri affirmamus*—an action may be right, but yet not expedient. The test of expediency is the "end" of the "Civil State," which is defined to be *pax vitaeque securitas,* and the life intended is one *quae maxime ratione, vera mentis virtute et vita, definitur.* In this doctrine Spinoza appeals not only to a different, but to an antagonistic set of motives. Man in a state of nature—*homo naturalis*—is unrelated, individual, atomic, except in so far as a state of conflict constitutes a relation. Man in Spinoza's "society"—*homo civilis*—is part of a larger whole, each member of which recognises a *common* good, maintained and fostered by mutual sympathy and harmonious action. Between these two conceptions is fixed an impassable gulf, and the word *jus*, correctly used of the latter status, is unmeaning in the phrase *jus naturale.*

But this misuse of the word *jus* brings out the cardinal error in Spinoza's *Politik,* viz., the belief in the possibility of a "right" in the individual apart from life in society. Spinoza failed to see that the conception "right" has meaning only in virtue of a function the individual performs relative to a certain end—this end being the common well-being of a society. "It is not in so far as I *can* do this or that, that I have a right to do this or that, but so far as I recognise myself and am recognised by others as able to do this or that for the sake of a common good."[1] Spinoza looked upon man, like everything else in Nature, as determined solely by material and efficient causes. As such, however, he has no rights or duties, but only "powers."

It is here that Plato and Aristotle are so much nearer the truth in their conception of the real end of the individual. To them man is φύσει πολιτικός—a phrase which asserts the doctrine of natural rights in the only sense in which it is true. But this teleological view of Society Spinoza ignores, and "in particular, he fails to notice that it is the consciousness of this τέλος to which his powers may be directed that constitutes the individual's claim to exercise them as rights, just as it is the recognition of them by a society as capable of such direction which renders them actually rights; in short that, just as according to him nothing is good or evil but thinking makes it so, so it is only thinking which makes a might a right—a certain conception of the

[1] *Pol. Oblig.* § 38.

might as relative to a social good on the part at once of the person exercising it, and of a society which it affects."[1]

(2) *Hobbes.*

The principle upon which Hobbes bases his political theory is identical with that of Spinoza. With him, too, men are at first *natura hostes*, and the only meaning of *jus naturale* is *potentia naturalis*. But Spinoza's teaching, in spite of a false start and an inconsistent development, contains fruitful elements which are entirely lacking in that of Hobbes. From Hobbes' central fiction—the sovereign person constituted by the social compact—with its consequences Spinoza keeps clear, not being influenced by Hobbes' desire to prove all resistance to established sovereignty unjustifiable.

But, doubly unsatisfactory as Hobbes' teaching is—both philosophically and historically—it enables us indirectly to gain a clearer conception of the nature of "Rights." The historical error of the social compact—implying as pre-existing just that state of things, a régime of recognised mutual obligations, it is presumed to account for—might have served to convey an important moral truth. It entirely fails, however, to do this, because it implies that individuals bring with them to the compact so-called "rights" which, apart from social function and social

[1] *Pol. Oblig.* § 41.

recognition, could "only be powers, *i.e.* they would not be rights at all; and from no combination or devolution of them could any right in the proper sense, anything more than a combined power, arise."[1]

(3) *Locke.*

Hobbes, Locke, and Rousseau differ only in their application of the same conception, which may be formulated as follows: "Men live first in a state of nature, subject to a law of nature, also called the law of Reason. In this state they are in some sense free and equal; but finding many inconveniences in it, they covenant with each other to establish a government—a covenant which they are bound by the 'law of nature' to observe—and out of this covenant the obligation of submission to the 'powers that be' arises."

In spite of the ambiguities in this doctrine, three points come out clearly.

(*a*) The conception of this pre-social state of nature is a purely *negative* one. It presents merely a state which was *not* one of political society—a state in which there was *no* civil government.

(*b*) Men were not only "equal," but in some mysterious and unexplained way they were also "free."

(*c*) They not only lived according to the law of

[1] *Pol. Oblig.* § 49.

nature, but were *conscious* of this law. They did not, perhaps, always obey it; but they recognised they *ought* to obey it.

To discuss the inconsistencies and impossibilities involved in each of these three points would be tedious, and is, fortunately for the present purpose, unnecessary. On (c) alone will it be helpful to dwell for a moment, for it is here the root error of the social contract theory—with its central fiction of rights attaching to pre-social men, and carried by them unimpaired into the new-born community—lies. This theory, whatever detailed shape be given to it, is always a ὕστερον πρότερον. The change, however brought about, from the old "freedom" to the new "order" is represented as an advance; but it would have been quite the reverse. A society, or to speak more accurately, a state of existence enjoyed by an indefinite number of individuals, of which it could be truly said that it was governed by a law of nature in the sense described—a society, *i.e.* of men, free and equal, recognising the mutual obligations implied in the "law," but free from the necessity of a sovereign or other coercive power to enforce its provisions—would be a society to which we look forward only as the final consummation of the educational processes involved in the history of civil government. In relation to it, ordinary political society is in an inferior stage of development. If thought of as actually succeeding it in time, it is a retrogression, not an advance. So far from freeing us from the "many inconveniences" of the state of nature, it chains and binds us with cords of our own making. In such a state of nature the need for civil government, for political organisation, disappears. The best political society we know only tries to realise imperfectly what is here represented as existing in perfection. As a matter of fact, this truth was recognised and brought out to a certain extent by Rousseau, with whom political society is a decline from a golden age.

The different application which Locke gave to the common theory (as compared with Hobbes) was due to the practical political objects they had respectively in view. Hobbes wished to condemn the Rebellion, Locke to justify the Revolution. Hence, Locke teaches that there remains ever in the hands of the Sovereign people a right to remove or alter the governing body, if it prove false to its trust. Unfortunately he left unanswered the important question, "What exactly is an act of the Sovereign people?"

On this point, too — the right to rebel — it is interesting to note how much truer the old Greek view was than these modern theories. The former deriving the obligation to political obedience, not from consent or some imaginary covenant, but from the end or function which the State served, obtained a rational justification for altering any government which failed to serve this "end," and which consequently became in technical language a παρέκβασις. Such failure, *eo ipso*, cancels all claim to obedience on the part of the citizens. This view involves, doubtless, practical difficulties of its own, but it at least gives, under definite conditions, a reasonable justification for resistance.

(4) *Rousseau.*

In Rousseau we have perhaps the best attempt to sketch a theory of political relationship in which individuals possess rights, inherent and unalienable, but without any corresponding duties. The keynote of his teaching lies in the turn of meaning he gave to the phrase "Sovereignty of the people." With Locke this sovereignty represents merely a power in reserve, to be exercised only in case the legislature prove false to its trust. Rousseau regards it as in constant exercise. The society does not *institute* a Sovereign, but in the act of formation *becomes* a Sovereign, and ever afterwards continues so.

From this act of formation arises a "collective moral body, composed of as many members as there are voices in the assembly, which body receives from this act its unity, its common self, its life, its will. It is called by its members a *state* when it is passive, a *sovereign* when it is active, a *power* when compared with similar bodies. The associates are called collectively a *people*, severally *citizens* as sharing in the sovereign authority, *subjects* as submitted to the laws of the state. Each of them is under an obligation in two relations—as a member of the sovereign body towards the individuals, and as a member of the state towards the sovereign. All the subjects can by a public vote be placed under a particular obligation towards the sovereign, but the sovereign cannot thus incur an obligation towards itself. It cannot impose any law upon itself which it cannot cancel. Nor is there need to restrict its powers in the interest of the subjects. For the sovereign body, being formed only of the individuals which constitute it, can have no interest contrary to theirs. From the mere fact of its existence, it is always all that it ought to be."[1]

In this association the individual "exchanges the natural liberty to do and get what he can ... for a liberty at once limited and secured by the general will; he exchanges the mere possession of such things as he can get, a possession which is the effect of force, for a property founded on a positive title, on the guarantee of society. At the same time he becomes a moral agent. Justice instead of instinct becomes the guide of his actions. For the moral slavery to appetite he substitutes the

[1] *Pol. Oblig.* § 66.

126 THE PHILOSOPHY OF T. H. GREEN

moral freedom which consists in obedience to a self-imposed law. Now for the first time it can be said that there is anything which he *ought* to do, as distinguished from that which he is *forced* to do."[1]

In this teaching Rousseau brings out a great truth, viz., That the real justification for a law or an act of government lies in the fact that it represents a true *volonté générale*—an impartial and disinterested will for the common good. Unfortunately, in practical application this ideal is (unavoidably) lost sight of. Confusion takes place between *volonté générale* and *volonté de tous*—in theory carefully distinguished by Rousseau—and the latter sinks into a mere quest for majorities. Rousseau makes a better attempt than any other writer to reconcile submission to a government with the existence of "natural" rights antecedent to the institution of government, but his results only show more clearly the hopelessness of the attempt. On the other hand, his conception of the State or Sovereign as representing a "general will" exercised for the common good, is of permanent value.

§ 3. THE BASIS OF THE STATE.

Historically a fiction Rousseau's doctrine is; but it has given us an essential truth, viz., that the State

[1] *Pol. Oblig.* § 67.

does represent in some way a "general will," which is a desire for a common good, and is the indispensable condition of its realisation. *Will, not force, is the basis of the State.* Not in a coercive authority imposed from without, but in a spiritual recognition, awakening and developing from within, is the efficient cause of the existence of a State to be found. Civic life lies in, and arises in response to, the conscious nature of man. But the political theorists we have been just considering fail to see this. With them, force — irresistible, coercive power — is, if not the origin, at least the sustaining factor, in the State. Force, too, exercised continually in opposition to individual liberty of effort and acquisition. The explanation of this error—from which even Rousseau himself is not free—is found in the erroneous assumption from which these writers start, or, to put it slightly differently, from their wrong method of framing the question to be solved. The two main elements in a State—sovereign and subject—are conceived of in too abstract a way. The subjects are looked upon, prior to their existence as such in a State, as persons possessed of natural rights, and endowed with social and moral attributes. On the other side stands, external and separate from them, a supreme coercive power which somehow they have to obey, and which is thought of as also the source of all law, all *jus*. Hence the obvious question, "Whence comes the 'right' of this supreme power to coerce and to guide individuals already possessing these natural rights and attributes?" This question, so stated, admits of no answer except by means of a *deus ex machinâ*, of some historical fiction, or other equally arbitrary device. No attempt, consequently, is made to ascertain how man *becomes* clothed with rights and duties. There is no real inquiry into the development of man in society. Throughout their whole teaching, in fact, runs the idea that force can *make* the State—an idea which both theoretically and practically is diametrically opposed to the truth.

The clue to the real basis of a State is to be found in the fact that there is "no right but thinking makes it so." A right is merely an idea which men have of each other. "Nothing is more real than a right, yet its existence is purely ideal, if by 'ideal' is meant that which is not dependent on anything material, but has its being solely in consciousness. It is to these ideal realities that force is subordinate in the creation and development of States."[1] Society begins in the consciousness of a common good, of common interests. These interests necessitate definite interrelations. It is recognised that order and organisation are part of the actual life of the community. Individuals become no longer atomic units, but integral parts of a (more or less dimly) recognised whole, clothed with various but appropriate rights

[1] *Pol. Oblig.* § 136.

and duties. Force, sovereign power, is in no sense the originator of these rights, though it co-operates in sustaining their regular performance. Every society is constituted and held together by a conscious, intelligent recognition of a common good. It is solely due to this recognition that individuals have attributes and rights; and the "power which in a political society they have to obey, is derived from the development and systematisation of those institutions for the regulation of a common life, without which they would have no rights at all."[1]

At this point certain thoughts may occur which may well give us pause. The theory just stated may be philosophically accurate, it may even be historically more or less correct (due allowance being made for the illusions of distance) of a small city-state of the time of Plato or Aristotle, but in what sense is it true of any modern State? Without coercive force would they exist for a day? Where does the "common good" come in as a motive compelling the ordinary citizen to, *e.g.*, pay house-rate or dog-tax? And how much influence did the conception exercise on those who, as a fact historically, founded the great European States of to-day? *Every society is constituted and held together by a conscious, intelligent recognition of a common good.* Such language, substituting "ought to be" for "is," may pass as an ethical ideal, but is surely mere

[1] *Pol. Oblig.* § 113.

delusion as explanation of the facts of the day? The "will of the individual" has seldom much to do with the demands of the State. It is true (to express the difficulty in detail) that "the necessity which the State lays upon the individual is for the most part one to which he is so accustomed that he no longer kicks against it; but what is it, we may ask, but an external necessity, which he no more lays on himself than he does the weight of the atmosphere, or the pressure of summer heat and winter frosts, that compels the ordinary citizen to pay rates and taxes, to serve in the army, to abstain from walking over the squire's fields, snaring his hares, or fishing in preserved streams, to pay rent, to respect those artificial rights of property which only the possessors of them have any obvious interest in maintaining, or even (if he is one of the 'proletariate') to keep his hands off the superfluous wealth of his neighbour, when he has none of his own to lose? Granted there are good reasons of social expediency for maintaining institutions which thus compel the individual to actions and forbearances that are none of his willing, is it not abusing words to speak of them as founded on a conception of general good? A conception does not float in the air. It must be somebody's conception. Whose conception, then, of general good is it that these institutions represent? Not that of most of the people who conform to them, for they do so because they are made to, or have come to do so habitually from having been long made to (*i.e.* from being frightened at the consequences of not conforming, not consequences which follow from not conforming in the ordinary course of nature, but consequences which the State inflicts, artificial consequences). But when a man is said to obey an authority from interest in a common good, some other good is meant than that which consists in escaping the punishment which the authority would inflict on disobedience. Is, then, the conception of common good which is alleged, a conception of it on the part of those who founded or who maintain the institutions in question? But is it not certain that private interests have been the main agents in establishing, and are still in maintaining, at any rate, all the more artificial rights of property? Have not our modern States, again, in nearly every case been founded on conquest, and are not the actual institutions of government in great measure the direct result of such conquest, or, where revolutions have intervened, of violence which has been as little governed by any conception of general good? Supposing that philosophers can find exquisite reasons for considering the institutions and requirements which have resulted from all this self-seeking and violence to be contributory to the common good of those who have to submit to them, is it not trifling to speak of them as founded on, or representing a conception of, this good, when no such conception has influenced those who established, maintain, or submit to them? And is it not seriously misleading when the requirements of the State have so largely arisen out of force directed by selfish motives, and when the motive to obedience to those requirements is determined by fear, to speak of them as having a common source with the morality of which it is admitted that the essence is to be disinterested and spontaneous?"[1]

These are grave objections which cannot be ignored. The difficulty is twofold, and may be formulated as follows:—

(*a*) The conception of a common good is not true of the ordinary citizen. His life (to his own mind) is ruled by the State as an "external necessity."

(*b*) A State cannot legitimately be said to exist to fulfil an idea which has had nothing to do with the actions which brought it into existence—as is the case with most States, *e.g.*, those due directly or indirectly to the action of Napoleon.

That these objections contain truth no one can deny, but the question is how much truth, and how far is it relevant to the point at issue. The "idea of a common good" has certainly seldom, if ever, been the *ruling* motive of those who, whether as agents or patients, have formed States. Yet a common good in some form—however imperfect or alloyed—

[1] *Pol. Oblig.* § 120.

has always been an essential element in the motive, and is so still. Without it no success beyond a temporary military dominion could have attended their efforts or produced acquiescence. Leaving for a moment the question of the principal agents, it is simple fact (in answer to objection *a*) that considerations of a common good, however limited in range, are the guiding influence of the ordinary citizen in his habitual obedience to civic institutions. Any claim he feels for his own "rights"—for wages, protection from outrage, fair dealing, &c., &c.—he feels only conditionally on his recognition of a like claim all round. The essence of such a claim lies in its being common to himself with others. That he does not see the bearing of every institution he lives under implies nothing more than that, being an ordinary citizen, his vision is limited. He is neither a great statesman nor a political philosopher, and doesn't understand the nature or relations of that which lies beyond his comprehension. But when he does recognise a common good, that recognition is the motive for his loyal obedience to the right maintained by law, and is the real factor which (in old Greek phrase) συνέχει τὴν πόλιν. Disloyalty, disobedience, disunion in the social whole arises when he sees that the "powers that be" are legislating for a class—for private, not public interests; when he perceives clearly that the State is *not* maintaining that which it is its sole function to maintain, viz., the rights and interests, common to himself and his neighbours, which he understands.

This recognition, again, as a rule, is not limited to the mere intellectual cognisance that this or that law is of common benefit. The citizen's feelings, his moral nature, are taken up into the life he lives in common with his fellows. He possesses a vote, he has a share in the making of the laws, both municipal and civic, he becomes habitually interested in the State as a whole (or at the very least, in a social community of some sort), and so widens the conceptions which otherwise might be confined to himself and his immediate neighbours, with their private rights. Lastly, feeling and habit, in the stricter sense of the term, quicken and transform these intelligent interests into living forces which guide and rule every department of his civic life. Common memories, common traditions, common language and literature, common religion, combine to strengthen and enrich that solidarity of himself with his fellow-citizens which issues (in its most obvious form) in the devoted patriotism ready to lay down its life for fatherland and fellow-countrymen.

We have still to deal with the second objection —that the founders of modern States were not actuated by the desire for a common good when they were "making history," but by very different motives, and that to regard a State as existing to fulfil an "end" which had nothing to do with the causes which brought it into existence, may be a "philosopher's dream," but is unmeaning in fact.

To this we have at first sight a tempting reply in the doctrine of evolution. The analogy between the life of a State and that of a natural organism is much to the front now-a-days, and offers ready and plausible help. All nature presents to us organisation and attainment of end of which there is no consciousness on the part of the organic agents themselves. Can we not argue in the same way that the State is "an organised community in the same sense in which a living body is, of which the members at once contribute to the function called life, and are made what they are by that function, according to an idea of which there is no consciousness on their part"?[1]

The objection to such a plea is simple, but sufficient. The State is not merely a natural, it is a moral organism. Its parts are human agents, actuated by motives, and working consciously for ends, however different sometimes the actual results may be from those originally aimed at. It is true that what are often called "natural accidents" have much to do with the demarcation of the several States, *e.g.* distribution of land

[1] *Pol. Oblig.* § 125.

and water, mountain ranges, &c., &c., but a State has a life and character of its own, due to very different agencies. A State is distinctively a "human" institution.

The question, then, is how far have such human agencies (as, *e.g.*, Napoleon I.), to whom the historical formation of many States is mainly due, been actuated by a conception of common good? Were not their motives purely selfish—desire for glory, personal ambition, and the like?

The answer is that, assuming the worst, *e.g.*, that Napoleon was actuated by a purely selfish passion for glory (if such a thing is even conceivable), yet to regard this by itself in abstraction as the "cause of the formation" of a State, is to commit a most serious mistake. The statement is true (if true at all) only with great modifications. His passion could only realise itself in the "greatness of France." It had to become absorbed in, and recognised by himself and others under this new and very different form, before it could begin to act as a factor in his work as conqueror and organiser. Further, this very greatness of France was conceived of as a moral power by the agents concerned. It meant to them the deliverance of oppressed peoples. They were fighting for the freedom of mankind, to secure for man his true inheritance. It is in these conceptions, in the concrete motive, not in any abstract relation to

Napoleon himself, that we must look for the real cause of the events in question. It is to this that the good out of evil, which we see resulting, is due. The evil represents the mischief produced by the alloy of selfishness, and the short-sightedness of political passion; the good was the direct object aimed at, the actual motive which became, more or less completely, realised in fact. Napoleon cannot be separated from the circumstances and character of the French people. It was not his selfishness, his idiosyncrasy, which moulded the institutions by which France, and other parts of Europe, have been civilised and developed; it was his fitness to act as an organ for the ideas which had obtained hold in society. These ideas, in their minds and in his, were ideas of common good. It is wrong to ignore such ideas because the chief instruments of their realisation may be, from one point of view, regarded as acting from selfish motives. Even in them the idea of a common good was a determining element—the element, in fact, to which alone their success in forming social institutions has been due.

The difficulty many thinkers find in recognising this truth, and the plausibility of the view that purely selfish passion has often been the cause of the formation of States, both arise from the error previously pointed out as characteristic of the "social contract" theorists, viz., the too exclusive attention given to the fact that a "supreme coercive power" is a necessity of a State's existence. This power, thought of abstractedly and separately, is regarded as the source of law and rights. It is forgotten that it is not the coercive power *as such* which makes a State; but that power combined with other factors, and exercised in a certain way, for a certain end. This end is the maintenance of definite legal institutions and social responsibilities. Not the Sovereign alone, nor even Sovereign and subjects aggregated together as two distinct entities, make the State; but Sovereign and citizens organised into a complex whole of inter-related responsibility. If we separate the two factors, it would be truer to say that the State makes the Sovereign, rather than the Sovereign the State. A slave-owner with his slaves, or the monarch of Persia (as depicted by Herodotus) and his subjects, do not make a State, for such despotic power is without the essential characteristic of a State, viz., a body of rights actually existing, which it is the function of sovereignty to guarantee and give full reality to. A Sovereign, in the ordinary political sense of the term, is in fact the final outcome of a process which takes a long time in its growth, and gradually incorporates many elements, none of which by themselves form a State, but which continue on unimpaired in the civic community. The State presupposes, and is in great part composed of, other narrower forms of community, *e.g.* family relationship, ties of clan and tribe. These relationships are taken up into the State, and formed into a "general law"; but this law does not abolish them, it gives them fuller reality under a supreme power, which "sustains, secures, and completes" them. The State is not, and can never be, a mere aggregate of individuals under a Sovereign.

This truth comes out clearly in cases, *e.g.* Russia with its autocratic Czar, which, if our theory is correct, can only be called States by courtesy. Even in these instances, the habitual obedience theoretically given solely to the arbitrary will of the despot is in reality given to something very different. It is due to the conviction that the rulings of the monarch are in accordance with the general interest of the people. If this conviction be shaken, the obedience becomes very far from habitual, and the State, in any intelligible sense of the term, disappears. It cannot be too often remembered that "the vast mass of influences, which we may call for shortness moral, perpetually shapes, limits, or forbids the actual direction of the forces of society by its Sovereign."[1] Only as the sustainer of the general will can the sovereign power claim or ensure habitual obedience. "Will, not force, is the basis of the State."

The State thus incorporates and secures rights— individual, family, tribal—which pre-exist, but which

[1] *Maine, Early Hist. of Inst.*, quoted *Pol. Oblig.* § 84.

"need definition and reconciliation in a general law. When such a general law has been arrived at, regulating the position of members of a family towards each other, and the dealings of families or tribes with each other; when it is voluntarily recognised by a community of families or tribes, and maintained by a power strong enough at once to enforce it within the community, and to defend the integrity of the community against attacks from without, then the elementary state has been formed."[1]

As it has been formed, so it grows. The very formation, with the administrative and other machinery it calls into being, gives rise to new relationships, new rights. Its existence renders possible (and actual) further relationships between man and man, which become more and more numerous and complex as society progresses. Each stage in the advance is based upon the previous one, and actuated by that idea of a common good to which greater definiteness is given as the "moralisation" of man (attainable only in civic life) increases and develops; but which from the earliest beginnings of common life has never been wholly absent.

§ 4. THE STATE AND THE INDIVIDUAL.

The citizen's life is made up of civic and social relations. Only as a "member of the State" has

[1] *Pol. Oblig.* § 134.

he any duties to perform, any rights to claim. All rights are due to his position as such a member, all his responsibilities consist in whatever is appropriate or necessary to the discharge of this function.

These considerations bring us face to face with the question hinted at in the first section of this chapter, viz., Has the individual no rights against the State? Does the "organic" analogy imply that acting as a member of the State cuts off for ever the possibility of acting as *he* thinks proper, as *he* likes? Does it leave him no more free than a part of any physical organism is free to act, if he thinks right, against the body corporate? And, if this is not the implication of our doctrine of "rights," under what circumstances, with what justification, is it "right" to protest or to rebel?

Theoretically and ideally, the answer to these questions is simplicity itself. The individual has *no* rights against the State. All rights flow from his position as a member of the State. If he ceases to be a member, if he cuts himself off and sets himself over against the State, he ceases *eo ipso* to have any rights at all. But this carries us a very little way. It emphasises the essential nature of a right, and reminds us that in the ideal society perfect freedom is only produced by perfect law, but is irrelevant to the point at issue. The question is not of theory, but of practice. It arises from the obvious matter-of-fact that no existing State is a perfectly organised whole, and no individual citizen without moral and intellectual shortcomings. Indeed, the difficulty arises sometimes from his very virtues. Man does, to his credit, love the highest when he sees it, and often finds the "powers that be" sustaining and fostering institutions which represent a stage of development far removed from what might be. From the beginning of political speculation, the question, "Can the good man be a good citizen?" has had a practical importance. Hence, there is no absurdity, but rather a pressing necessity to ask, "Under what circumstances is it right to rebel, *i.e.* to act in opposition to State authority?"

One general rule (perhaps the only one) is clear, viz., there can be "no right to disobey the law of the State except in the interest of the State."[1] At first sight this may seem too general to be of any practical use, but a little reflection shows that it is not so. It puts out of Court at once all pleadings against beneficial legislation, *e.g.* Factory or Education Acts, based upon a supposed individual right to do what he likes with his own, or to have his freedom untampered with, &c., &c. But it carries us much further than this—it confines within the narrowest limits the right to disregard, or even protest against, legislation which seems the reverse of beneficial. It means (in practical application) that the citizen has

[1] *Pol. Oblig.* § 142.

no right to rebel, against presumably unjust laws, arbitrarily on a supposed right to do as he thinks fit, but that he has counter rights (rights of opposition) against such enactments only if he fulfil two conditions, viz. :

(*a*) if he can point to a definite social good to be gained by successful opposition.

(*b*) if this social good is one recognised as such by his fellow-citizens. He must show, conclusively to their minds as well as his, that the enactments in question are in the interests of a class at the expense of the general well-being, and so plead against the State in the true interest of the State.

The last point—the true interest of the *State*—is the most important consideration, and at the same time the one most easily lost sight of. It is comparatively easy—in the imperfectly organised States we know—to convince ourselves and many of our fellow-citizens that this or that enactment is unjust—that it fosters the interests of a class (to which we do not belong)—that it is injurious to the well-being of the State, and so forth. The conclusion "Let us disregard it" follows easily and plausibly, but what is the motive for the disobedience? If it is the "well-being of the State," good, but may it not be our own private interest? Two wrongs do not make a right, however much the existence of the first may provide extenuating circumstances for the second. The revenue laws, a generation or two ago, in

England were economically unsound, and may be admitted, for argument's sake at least, to have been[1] advantageous to a small class at the expense of the community at large, but it is to be feared that the practice of smuggling was due to motives which had little to do with that idea of the good of the State which alone justifies disobedience to State Enactment. The smugglers represented that war of class against class, or rather that "fighting for one's own hand," which, if logically carried out, destroys the common weal altogether. The secret sympathy with which even Revenue officers regarded the practice was due to the general conviction of the injustice of certain enactments, and was consistent with the most devoted loyalty to the State in other references, but the motives as a fact actuating both smugglers and buyers render the practice impossible of moral justification. Only when, confessedly and obviously, acting in the true interest of the State, is it right to act against the State.

Now the one fundamental interest of the State is that each citizen should cheerfully perform his function as such, *i.e.*, should act in accordance with his social relations with as clear and wide conception of these relations, and how they serve the common

---

[1] *Cf.* Works, vol. ii. p. 484. "All restrictions on freedom of wholesome trade are really based on special class interests, and must disappear with the realisation of that individual right, founded on the capacity of every man for free contribution to social good, which is the true idea of the State."

good, as is compatible with his intelligence and station. The parts of the body politic, though organic to social life, are not parts of a physical body. They are living persons—free agents. Only in so far as they are capable of realising the conception of a common good, and are free to act as they see the common good requires, can they perform their duties as citizens. Hence, from the standpoint of the individual, one "right" stands out pre-eminent and fundamental, viz., the right to life and liberty, or (in the phrase Green prefers) the "right to free life."

This is the *sine quâ non* of citizenship. It is possessed by all who have the capacity for membership of a society, *i.e.* who are capable of determining their actions by reference to a good common to themselves and others. No social polity which denies the actualisation of this right to any class of men so qualified can represent more than a temporary phase of development. Hence the objection to slavery. This institution may be at first an advance upon a practice which previously obtained, *e.g.* total extirpation; it may have been a necessary stage in a nation's growth, but it can form no part of a settled or permanent constitution, δοκεῖ γὰρ εἶναι τι δίκαιον παντὶ ἀνθρώπῳ πρὸς πάντα τὸν δυνάμενον κοινωνῆσαι νόμου καὶ συνθήκης,[1] and slavery, logically and theoretically, is a denial of this

[1] Arist. *N.E.* viii. 11.

"natural" right. As a matter of fact it is never logically carried out in practice, but nevertheless it is necessarily a partial withholding from a class of individuals rights to which they are by nature entitled; entitled, that is, by the actual possession of the faculty qualifying for citizenship. This right to free life can only be lost by, and is only justly denied to, those who show themselves <u>incapable of</u> the idea of <u>common good</u> and of self-determination by it; *i.e.* by lunatics or criminals.

On the other hand, the right to free life has definite limitations and determinations. No one would deny that the State has rights of interference with the individual liberty, even of capable citizens, in many directions; rights which are not theoretical merely, but daily acted upon. The explanation, or justification, of these rights of the State against the individual is necessarily identical with that for the rights of the individual against the State, viz., the well-being of the community as a whole. Whatever is directly of service in producing the "citizen" (assuming its practical possibility) is right to be carried out in civic life, and ought to be objectified in some law or institution. It sometimes happens in the discharge of this strictly State function that the government seems, not only to interfere with supposed rights of individuals, but also to usurp their moral responsibilities; to arrogate to itself a duty incumbent upon the private citizen, and which he ought to be left to perform. Compulsory education, for example, has been objected to, not only by selfish parents enraged that their power to exploit the labour of their little ones is taken away, but also on the ethical ground that to care for the spiritual, as well as physical, welfare of children, is a moral duty attaching to the parent, from which, consequently, he ought not to be relieved, and, as a fact, cannot be relieved except at the expense of lowering the moral life of the individual. This argument would have weight if the State's motive were merely to take upon its own shoulders a moral responsibility more naturally belonging to the individual, or, if it enforced the " sending the child to school " as a moral duty which the parent must be compelled to perform. But the motive of the State is a very different one. Its object is simply to prevent a hindrance (certain to be there unless the State interferes) to the development of the capacity for civic rights on the part of the children. Without this interference on the part of the State, the children would never grow into capable citizens at all. It is as sustainer and enforcer of rights the State acts, not as a moral teacher. In so acting it is strictly fulfilling its own function, not attempting to carry the burdens of others.

So, too, with other State interferences, each of which must be judged separately on its own merits by the above criterion. The action of government is primarily negative. Laws regulating hours of labour for women and children, confining tenant right in Ireland, limiting freedom of contract, and the like, are not rightly regarded if taken to be positive rulings of men's actions in certain definite ways. They do, indirectly, have this effect doubtless, but, directly, their function is to remove hindrances to the growth of civic capacity on the part of individuals, or classes of individuals, who otherwise would never have the chance of that "free life" which it is the one essential function of the State to secure for every citizen.

Of these rights of State interference — too numerous to enter into in detail — there is one which demands consideration, both from its importance and from certain characteristics it possesses peculiar to itself; viz., the right of the State to punish.

This State right is really the correlative of the right of the individual to free life, *so long as* he is contributory to the general good. Conversely, the civic association has necessarily the right to prevent such actions as tend to destroy, on the part of other citizens, freedom of action contributory to social well-being. The criminal interferes with the exercise of legitimate rights by his fellows — the State, in the discharge of its proper function, interferes with this interference by laying violent hands upon the offender. By this exercise of authority a stop is put to his acting altogether—so far, that is, as the social sphere is concerned.

In answer, then, to the old controversy as to the nature of punishment—ought it to be preventive, retributive, or reformatory—it is clear that, *primarily*, punishment is preventive. It is directed towards the removal of hindrances; it regards the interest of law-abiding citizens, not the depravity of the law-breaker; it "clears the course." This object is effected by associating with wrong action a certain amount of terror—terror sufficient to divert a would-be wrong-doer from his purpose. On the other hand, though *primarily* preventive, it is not *merely* preventive. This is the confusion of thought which breeds the tyrant and oppressor, not the judge. Not any amount of terror is justifiable because it happens to "prevent." The punishment should never go beyond what is actually necessary to associate with the crime, in order to prevent the violation of the right its intention is to preserve from interference. The idea of retribution is an essential, though not the primary, element in punishment. Retribution not, of course, in the sense in which pre-social private vengeance is retributive—private vengeance is the polar opposite of State punishment, which gradually suppresses it and takes its place—but as expressing the sympathetic *public* indignation which is felt at beholding wrong-doing, even when inflicted on others. "This indignation is inseparable from the interest in social well-being, and along with it is the chief agent in the establishment and maintenance of legal punishment."[1] We feel the criminal ought to be treated according to his deserts, "ought to have his due." This conception of "justly due" or "retributively just" is a most valuable corrective to the danger of falling into the "merely preventive" theory. It implies a two-fold recognition—both on the part of the criminal, and also by society—of the act done as wrong, and the punishment inflicted as fitting. "The idea of punishment implies on the side of the person punished . . . a practical understanding of the nature of rights, and an actual violation of a right or omission to fulfil an obligation, the right or obligation being one of which the agent might have been aware, and the violation or omission one which he might have prevented. On the side of the authority punishing, it implies equally a conception of right founded on relation to public good, and one which, unlike that on the part of the criminal, is realised in act; a conception of which the punitive act, as founded on a consideration of what is necessary for the maintenance of rights, is the logical expression. A punishment is unjust if either element is absent; if either the

[1] *Pol. Oblig.* § 183.

act punished is not a violation of known rights or an omission to fulfil known obligations of a kind which the agent might have prevented, or the punishment is one that is not required for the maintenance of rights."[1]

"Maintenance of rights"—this phrase cannot be too much emphasised. The function of legal punishment, as both preventive and retributive, is definitely the protection of rights, not the castigation of moral depravity as such. The State is the sustainer of rights. It has regard, not to the wickedness of the criminal, but to the effect of the punishment on others. It looks forward, not backwards. No punishment can prevent the crime accomplished—it can only try to render less likely the doing of a similar wrong in the future. Herein lies the true justification of "extenuating circumstances." These can be always legitimately pleaded (and acted upon) whenever the lightening of a punishment "justly" attached to the right violated does not, in the particular case in question, weaken the deterrent association in the minds of others. An odd case of, *e.g.* a starving man snatching at a loaf, may be lightly dealt with without fear of promoting in the community a general disrespect for the eighth commandment. But in a beleaguered city the same act might, from exactly the same considerations, "justly" require the punishment of death; in no

[1] *Pol. Oblig.* § 185.

other way could the rights of the others be preserved from violation.

There are, in fact, two good and sufficient reasons why punishment should *not* be apportioned to the "moral wickedness"[1] of the wrong-doer:—

(*a*) The degree of moral depravity implied in a crime is unascertainable. It depends on the motive and character. It is unknown fully even to the individual himself, and cannot be estimated by an external judge.

(*b*) It is not the business of the State to punish wickedness, as such. Indirectly, punishment serves a moral purpose; but its prime object is to secure opportunity for the performance of social function on the part of the body of the citizens. "There is no direct reference in punishment by the State, either retrospective or prospective, to moral good or evil. The State in its judicial action does not look to the moral guilt of the criminal whom it punishes, or to the promotion of moral good by means of his punishment in him or others. It looks not to virtue and vice, but to rights and wrongs. It looks back to the wrong done in the crime which it punishes; not, however, in order to avenge it, but in order to the consideration of the sort of terror which needs to be associated with such wrong-doing, in order to the future maintenance of rights. If the character of the criminal comes into account at all,

[1] *Pol. Oblig.* § 196.

it can only be properly as an incident of this consideration."[1]

In actual result, however, the "character of the criminal" is affected; and reflection shows us that punishment, to be really preventive, must be reformatory. It must tend to "qualify the criminal for the resumption of rights."[2] Though not aiming at the moral good of the criminal as its ultimate end, it strives to refit him for taking his place as a citizen, with renewed capacity and fresh determination to fulfil his social responsibilities. In this way a definite limitation of the amount and kind of punishment which the State can legitimately inflict arises. The criminal himself has rights which must be respected. Not rights in the sense of the word when applicable to his fellow law-abiding citizens. He has *eo ipso* forfeited these, and is, for the time being, "out of" civic and social relations. His rights are potential, or, so to speak, "reversionary"; but they are real, and he must not be for ever incapacitated for the resumption of them.

To this rule there is one exception—the penalty of death, or what is the same thing from the standpoint of civic rights, that of life imprisonment. These extreme penalties may be justified on either (or both) of two grounds:—

[1] *Pol. Oblig.* § 204. [2] *Ibid.* § 206.

(*a*) Association of extremest terror may be necessary with certain actions to preserve the possibility of social life at all.

(*b*) The crime punished may of itself show the criminal to be permanently incapable of the exercise of rights.[1]

In the case of the penalty of death for murder —and possibly some other crimes—both justifications may be urged.

---

[1] *Pol. Oblig.* § 205.

CHAPTER VII.

GREEN AND HIS CRITICS

THESE lectures, so far, have been expository in the literal sense of the term. They have tried to reproduce Green's teaching—often in his own words—without any attempt at criticism. The aim of this concluding chapter is to supplement this direct exposition by examining the chief criticisms which have been brought against his teaching.

It is so obvious that the Moral and Political portions of this teaching stand, or fall, with the truth, or untruth, of the Metaphysics that, strictly speaking, it is wasted labour to either attack or defend any ground not covered by *Prolegomena* Bk. I., but I have thought it better, for practical purposes, to add some account of Professor Sidgwick's objections to the doctrine contained in the later books. The published criticisms of Green are not numerous, but the difficulties they raise are fundamental. The best statement of them is to be found, undoubtedly, in the first, and the concluding, chapters of Professor Seth's *Hegelianism and Personality*. Of this statement I have given a full and, I trust, impartial summary, to which I have added a slighter sketch of Mr. Balfour's article in *Mind* (January, 1884), and an analysis of Professor Sidgwick's article in the following number (April, 1884). Some answer to these criticisms was also obviously required, but I have tried to keep this within the narrowest possible compass, by dealing only with the more important issues raised.

§ 2. *Professor Seth's Criticism.* "Green's whole system centres in the assertion of a Self or Spiritual Principle, as necessary to the existence alike of Knowledge and Morality. The presence of this principle of connection and unity to the particulars of sense, alone renders possible a cosmos or intelligible world, and is likewise the sole explanation of Ethics as a system of precepts. The impressive assertion of this one position may . . . almost be said to constitute his entire system."[1]

The critical part of this teaching (*i.e.* as against the sensationalism of Hume, &c.) may be accepted as "victorious and conclusive," but in the positive teaching as to the nature of the Self or Spiritual Principle everything is left vague and ambiguous. It is nowhere explained how the individual self is a reproduction of a divine universal self, and

[1] *Hegelianism*, p. 4.

what evidence there is for the possibility of this relation of identification.

The ambiguity which thus clings to Green's central position is due to the source from which he derived it, viz., the Kantian philosophy read in the light of the Hegelian system.[1] This development possessed a radical flaw. Kant's method of proof is the analysis of experience with a view to discover its indispensable constitutive elements.[2] Taking the fact of knowledge as it finds it, it does not inquire how that fact was realised or came into being . . . but, *moving always within the fact*, it asks what are the conditions of its being what it is—what, in other words, are its essential elements? It is an analysis of the *nature* of knowledge, not of its *genesis*.

This method has its limitations; it can only give us a theory of knowledge and not a ready-made ontology—it is not an absolute theory of the universe.[3] Herein lies Green's great mistake. He claims to follow out the transcendental method to its legitimate issue, and make Kant consistent with himself, but in so doing he avowedly transforms Kant's theory of knowledge into a metaphysic of existence, an absolute philosophy. It is this transformation which forms the core of the Neo-Kantian position. Green explicitly identifies the self which the theory of knowledge reveals

[1] *Hegelianism*, p. 5. [2] *Ibid.* p. 16. [3] *Ibid.* p. 21.

—the single, active, self-conscious principle—with the universal or divine self-consciousness, the one eternal divine subject to which the universe is relative, and which makes the animal organism of man a vehicle for the reproduction of itself.[1]

Now this conversion of "consciousness in general, without more ado, into a universal consciousness is in the highest degree improper. The transcendental theory of knowledge, because it is an abstract inquiry, necessarily speaks of a single self or logical subject; but this singularity is the singularity which belongs to every abstract notion, and decides nothing as to the singularity or plurality of existing intelligences. We can have absolutely no right to transform this logical identity of type into a numerical identity of existence. Yet this seems to be precisely the step which Neo-Kantism makes. It takes the notion of knowledge as equivalent to a real knower, and the form of knowledge being one, it leaps to the conclusion that what we have before us is the one subject who sustains the world, and is the real Knower in all finite Intelligences. This is neither more nor less than to hypostatise an abstraction. It is of a piece with the Scholastic Realism which hypostatised *humanitas*, or *homo*, as a universal substance of which individual men were the accidents. Green's theory of the universe may be

[1] *Hegelianism*, p. 23.

true, but its truth must be established upon other lines."[1]

Professor Seth holds, lastly, Green's doctrine of the self to be not only illegitimate and unproven, but also self-destructive—it destroys, *i.e.*, both man and God. In his own words: "The radical error, both of Hegelianism and of the allied English doctrines, I take to be the identification of the human and the divine self-consciousness, or . . . the unification of consciousness into a single self. It is true there could be no interaction between individuals, unless they were all embraced within one Reality; still less could there be any knowledge by one individual of others if they did not all form parts of one system of things. But it is a great step further to say that this universal attitude of the self, as such, is due to the fact that it is one universal self that thinks in all so-called thinkers . . . for each self is a unique existence which is perfectly *impervious* to other selves—impervious in a fashion, of which the impenetrability of matter is a faint analogue . . . It is none the less true, of course, that only through selfhood am I able to recognise the unity of the world, and my own union with the source of all . . . but though the self is thus in knowledge a principle of unification, it is in existence, or metaphysically, a principle of isolation. There is no deliverance of consciousness which is more unequivocal than that

[1] *Hegelianism*, p. 29.

160 THE PHILOSOPHY OF T. H. GREEN

which testifies to this independence and exclusiveness. I have a centre of my own—a will of my own—which no one shares with me, nor can share—a centre which I maintain even in my dealings with God Himself," but "Green's doctrine of the universal self is a thorough-going Pantheism."[1] In fact, "the attempt of the Hegelian and Neo-Hegelian schools to unify the human and divine subject is ultimately destructive of the reality of both[2] ... if we are to keep the name God at all, subjectivity—an existence of God for Himself, analogous to our own personal existence, though doubtless transcending it infinitely in innumerable ways—is an essential element in the conception. We can only know Him as manifested in Nature and history; and knowledge of the manifestation is in both cases knowledge of the essence ... but just as the man has a centre of his own, so, if we speak of God at all, there must be a divine centre of thought, activity, and enjoyment to which no mortal can penetrate ... Moreover, the admission of a real self-consciousness in God seems demanded of us if we are not to be unfaithful to the fundamental principle of the theory of knowledge—interpretation by means of the highest category within our reach ... God *may*, nay, *must* be, infinitely more—we are at least certain that he cannot be less—than we know ourselves to be."[3]

So far Professor Seth—his last sentences sound

[1] *Hegelianism*, p. 215-218.   [2] *Ibid.* p. 222.   [3] *Ibid.* p. 224.

strange in our ears as a *criticism* of Green's teaching —they are, in fact, a (presumably unconscious) reproduction of an essential portion of it. Compare, *e.g.*, § 182 of the *Prolegomena:* "It is clearly of the very essence of our doctrine that the divine principle, which we suppose to be realising itself in man, should be supposed to realise itself in persons, as such. But for reflection on our personality, on our consciousness of ourselves as objects to ourselves, we could never dream of their being such a self-realising principle at all . . . It is the irreducibility of this self-objectifying consciousness to anything else, the impossibility of accounting for it as an effect, that compels us to regard it as the presence in us of the mind for which the world exists. To admit, therefore, that the self-realisation of the divine principle can take place otherwise than in a consciousness which is an object to itself, would be in contradiction of the very ground upon which we believe that a divine principle does so realise itself in man. Personality, no doubt, is a term that has often been fought over without any very precise meaning being attached to it. If we mean anything else by it than the quality in a subject of being consciously an object to itself, we are not justified in saying that it necessarily belongs to God . . . But whatever we mean by personality, and whatever difficulties may attach to the notion that a divine principle realises itself . . . in the persons of men, it is certain we shall only fall into contradictions by substituting for persons ... any entity to which self-consciousness cannot intelligibly be ascribed. If it is impossible that the divine self-realisation should be complete in such persons as we are ... on the other hand, in the absence of self-objectification—the essential thing in personality—it cannot even be inchoate."

Such quotations may be easily multiplied, but it is needless to do so. They bring out a curious misunderstanding, common to all the metaphysical (at least) criticism of Green's teaching, viz., that he is Pantheistic. As a consequence, a large portion of so-called "criticism" is not only a "beating the air," but reproduces, more forcibly perhaps and eloquently than Green's severely scientific style admits, the very doctrine the *Prolegomena* was written to teach us. But before attempting to answer our critics, it will be better to hear Mr. Balfour.

§ 3. Mr. Balfour—in *Mind*, January, 1884—fastening upon the word Neo-Kantian, describes Green's Metaphysic as a "simplified Kantism, purged of things-in-themselves, and denuded of the complicated architectonic structure with which its first author encumbered it."[1] Whereas, however, Kant held that a scientific knowledge of phenomena alone is possible, Green "professes to demonstrate the existence of individual self-conscious spirits outside the realm of phenomena altogether, and of one universal self-

[1] Page 76.

conscious Spirit, through which alone the world of phenomena exists, and of which all other intelligences are the imperfect manifestations." Mr. Balfour then urges, in his clear-cut and trenchant manner, the same objections just quoted from Professor Seth (which it is obviously unnecessary to repeat), describing Green's doctrine as a Pantheism, in which it is "as true to say that the world created God, as that God created the world," and emphasising the fact that the "self" individualises and isolates, &c. Finally, pointing out with perfect truth that Green has not really *explained* how the relation he supposes between the human self and God is possible, or even adequately conceivable by us, he complains that Green thus gives us theological mysteries rather than philosophical conclusions, though he is kind enough to add that the attempt is not "discreditable," for after all "we are human beings, and not investigating machines." In *Mind* for October, 1893, he repeats —substituting the word "mysticism" for "theology" —his earlier essay in a more popular form.

§ 4. On the whole these two criticisms agree with each other, and exhaust the difficulties which, as yet, have been brought forward against Green's main teaching. There is, however, one point peculiar to Mr. Balfour upon which it is important to pause for a moment, viz., the confusion between *science* and *omniscience*. There are problems still left *un-explained* by Green, therefore his analysis, *as far as it goes*, must be incorrect. This argument is a *non sequitur* which more than once appears in modern philosophical writing—especially critical writing. It is easy to bring forward, dangerously misleading to the reader, and, to say the least of it, hopelessly irrelevant. It may be going too far to urge that "the non-attainment of finality in a philosophy is its highest virtue"; but these words are merely an exaggeration of a great truth. Human knowledge cannot be "final." If it professes to be so, it condemns itself as one-sided and incomplete. The question to ask is, "Is its analysis of the facts of which we are conscious correct as far as it goes?" If it omits some of these admitted facts, or is self-contradictory in its explanations, it must be rejected; but if we *can* find a theory of metaphysics not open to these objections, and whose sole shortcoming it is that it fails to give us an "adequate conception" of what things will look like when we *are* all we may ultimately *become*, we are bound as rational beings to give in our adherence to that theory. To admit that a philosopher is on the right road is to admit everything; to complain that he has not yet reached the goal is puerile. In regard to this special accusation of "theological mystery," Green has argued simply that certain facts—universally admitted—necessitate certain other facts, *e.g.* God; but he very properly declines to specify further qualities in Him, not so necessitated. This is not to leave us a "mystery"—it is merely to refrain from the foolish attempt to "adequately explain" where we are without the requisite *data*.

Coming now to the critical estimate common to Professor Seth and Mr. Balfour, it will be found to fall naturally into three parts:—

(1) That portion of it which endorses and agrees with certain aspects of Green's teaching.

(2) Those positions and arguments in support which, though by a misunderstanding they are brought forward as criticism, are really a reproduction of his doctrine, and would have been cordially endorsed by him.

(3) A third portion, which is really criticism, but is based upon unconscious misrepresentation.

Let us consider these separately.

Green represents what may be called Integration, as opposed to Disintegration—both in Thought and Being. This negative, controversial side of his teaching has a value which is fully recognised by our critics. As against Disintegration, he is "victorious and conclusive." The mind is not, as Hume and Mill maintain, a series of disconnected, successive, atomic sensations or ideas; nature is no aggregate of phenomena objectively corresponding to such ideas—it is a whole of parts. Green, with his (supposed) master, Kant, has established once and for all the validity of the logical and moral "self." Negatively, then, Green is satisfactory; and we may pass at once to the positive side of his teaching.

The point upon which both Professor Seth and Mr. Balfour insist, at so great length and with so much emphasis, is that the self, once obtained, must be retained. No theory which absorbs this self into something other or higher can be accepted. Man has a "centre of his own," which is maintained even in his "dealings with God himself." Such a centre, though "infinitely transcending" the human in innumerable ways, is an essential element in the conception of God. "God may—nay, must be—infinitely more—we are at least certain that he cannot be less—than we know ourselves to be."

As one reads this language, it is difficult to avoid a feeling of helpless bewilderment. Are the words "critic" and "plagiarist" interchangeable terms? For assuredly that portion of Seth's book, from which I have just quoted a few phrases, consists literally of the reproduction of teaching which Green enunciates, reiterates, and supports, in every way he can, throughout the greater part of the *Prolegomena*. The § 182, quoted *supra*, does not stand alone. The whole gist of his utterances upon the nature of the Self—both divine and human—upon the personal character of the Moral Ideal, upon reformation of character, &c., &c., has for its very kernel the truth that "no deliverance of consciousness is so unequivocal" as that which testifies that man *is* a "Self" in all his being and doing—from the simplest sensation to the highest complexity of thought. No metaphysical theory of existence, no ethical dream of a far-off ideal, in which this individual selfhood is obscured or transformed into something else, would have been accepted—still less taught—by Green for a moment. It is useless to add more on this head. Let us consider, thirdly, the critical portion proper of Professor Seth's book. This will be found to be based upon a misunderstanding of Green's method, owing to which Seth seems to think that Green began with his final conclusion, or, in other words, based his whole theory upon a gratuitously assumed conception, which is really the final result to which his reasoning forced him.

Green establishes the validity of the "Logical Self"; but instead of using this Logical Self when he has got it, he abuses it. The whole pith of the Seth-Balfour objections lies in the words, "We have absolutely no right to transform a logical identity of type into a numerical identity of existence—to make a theory of knowledge into a ready-made ontology." Whether this feat be even a possible one it is useless to enquire, for it is certain that Green does not attempt it. The only "ready-made" element in his system is the assumption (made by all constructive science) that knowledge is possible, and the only "ontology" he begins with his own existence. "What have I got in my head, and what is the simplest explanation of it?" are the questions he asks. His relation to Kant consists in a grateful acknowledgment of that philosopher's doctrine that experience involves for its possibility a permanent self, together with an emphatic warning not to follow him in "asserting the unity of the world of our experience only to transfer that world to a larger chaos." The phrase, Neo-Kantian, is in the highest degree unfortunate. Professor Seth admits, it is true, that "Neo-Kantism is as different from Kant as Neo-Platonism from Plato"; and Mr. Balfour perceives "that the most Kantian of recent transcendentalists would probably never have been described by Kant himself as his disciples";[1] but apparently Neo-Kantism must be either a copy or a corruption of Kant, and as it is not the former, it must be condemned as the latter. Hence the use of words like "illegitimate," "ready-made," "without more ado," "transformation," "conversion," &c., &c. Once admit, however, the possibility that Green's doctrine is the result of an independent investigation, and the irrelevancy of these reproaches becomes obvious. The simple truth is that the "Self" Green starts with is neither logical nor ontological in any significant sense—it is just "his own self." From this, in order to explain it and its attributes, he finds himself driven step by step with irresistible cogency to the

[1] Page 73.

cosmos, and from that to God. The "universal Knower" of which Seth complains so much (as an assumption) is not Green's starting-point; it is the final conclusion, to which he is led by the "best analysis he can make" of his own experience. Do our critics object to this analysis? They name it "victorious and conclusive." Do they point out missing links in the chain—a long chain, remember —by which we reach the "eternal consciousness"? They ignore it altogether, and assume that Green starts with his ultimate conclusion. No wonder, then, viewing the doctrine as such a monstrous *petitio principii*, they urge that, "if true, its truth must be established on other lines." Yet the other part of their misunderstanding is, perhaps, even worse. This illegitimate, ontological "Self" is not even personal—Green's philosophy is a "thoroughgoing Pantheism," of a piece with the "crude scholastic realism which hypostatised *humanitas*," &c., &c. It is, indeed, difficult to attempt seriously to answer such an *ignoratio elenchi* as this. Green is, doubtless, open to criticism; but any criticism worthy of serious consideration must assuredly be "upon other lines." As against such misrepresentation, it may be fairly urged that Green's starting-point and method of procedure are legitimate; that his analysis, while giving us facts which we recognise in our own experience, nowhere drags in elements not apparently necessitated by these facts; that the structure gradually built up is consistent with itself; and that finally the difficulties remaining—to complete the metaphysical solution—show as yet no indication that they will require treatment by other methods. These "difficulties" are practically two, viz. :—

(1) How is it that the, as yet, unknown elements in a spiritual universe *appear* material?

(2) How is it possible for several individual selves —whether human or divine—to be all of them parts of *one* cosmos?

It is both a privilege and a duty to work away at these questions; it is irrational to blame a predecessor who saw them as clearly as we do, that he did not live long enough to reach them. Green tells us clearly what he starts with, how he proceeds, the conclusions he arrives at. That these conclusions, or some of them, are startling, he frankly admits, that no "adequate conception" of *one* of them in its full reality is as yet humanly possible he emphatically urges, but holds — and surely legitimately holds—that till his theory "can be shown to have left some essential part of the reality of the case out of sight, and another conclusion can be substituted for it which remedies the defect, this is no reason for rejecting it."[1] The criticisms above-quoted make no attempt to show any such gap or inconsistency in Green's analysis.

[1] *Proleg.* § 82.

Still less do they substitute a theory which remedies that or any other defect. It is scarcely unfair to say that, when not engaged in reproducing, with eloquence all their own, Green's main doctrine, they busy themselves with bursts of righteous indignation against a crude ontology which, whatever its source, assuredly cannot be found in any extant edition of Green's writings.

§ 5. *Professor Sidgwick's criticism*, vide "Mind," April, 1884. Professor Sidgwick finds himself "unable to put together into a coherent whole the different expressions of Green's ethical view"[1] found in the *Prolegomena of Ethics.*

"Green's doctrine as to the basis of morality, in the most comprehensive account which he gives of it, is stated to be a 'Theory of the Good as Human Perfection.' The Perfection which is thus taken as the ultimate end of rational conduct, is otherwise described as the 'realisation,' 'development,' or 'completion' of human 'faculties' or 'capabilities.' If we ask, further, to what part of man's apparently composite nature these 'faculties' or 'capabilities' belong, we are told that they are 'capabilities of the spirit which is in man,' to which, again, a 'divine' or 'heaven-born' nature is attributed. The realisation of these capabilities is, in fact, a 'self-realisation of the divine principle in man'; that is, of the 'one

[1] *Mind*, vol. ix. p. 169.

divine mind,' which 'gradually reproduces itself in the human soul.' 'God,' we are elsewhere told, 'is a Being with whom the human spirit is identical, in the sense that He *is* all which the human spirit is capable of becoming.' Hence the conception of the Divine Spirit presents to the man who is morally aspiring, an 'ideal of personal holiness' with which he contrasts his own personal unworthiness."

This doctrine, if it is to give us anything more than a "vague, emotional thrill," must be expressed in much more definite form and, in particular, must answer distinctly two questions, viz. :—

(1) "How is this relation of man to God philosophically known?"

(2) "What definite and reasoned content can be given to this notion of a Divine Spirit?"

"An answer to these questions was intended, apparently, to be given in Book I. . . . Here we are certainly introduced to a 'spiritual principle in nature,' corresponding to the spiritual principle implied in all human knowledge or experience. It is argued that to constitute the 'single, all-inclusive, unalterable system of relations' which we find in nature, properly understood, something beyond nature is needed: 'something which renders all relations possible,' and supplies the 'unity of the manifold' which is involved in the existence of these relations. 'A plurality of things cannot of themselves unite in one relation, nor can a single thing of itself bring itself into a multitude of relations . . . there must be something other than the manifold things themselves which combines them.' Such a 'combining agency' in each one's experience is his own intelligence, his intelligent self which unites the objects of his experience while distinguishing itself from them. Hence, if we suppose nature to be real, 'otherwise than merely as for us,' we must 'recognise as the condition of this reality the action of some unifying principle analogous to that of our understanding.' Indeed, Green passes—I do not precisely understand how—from the affirmation of *analogous action* to the affirmation of *identical quality*, and says that nature in its reality implies not only an all-uniting agency which is not natural, but a thinking, self-distinguishing consciousness like our own. We further find that this principle of synthesis or unity is 'eternal,' in the sense that it is not in time, and 'complete,' in the sense that its combining agency extends to all conceivable objects; and that our own empirical knowledge can only be explained as an imperfect reproduction in us of this eternally complete consciousness."[1]

"But how . . . . can we possibly get an 'ideal of holiness,' of an 'infinitely and perfectly good will,' out of this conception of a combining, self-

[1] *Mind*, p. 171.

distinguishing and self-objectifying agency?" The only perfection the human spirit, as the reproduction of such an agency, can aim at, is the increase of knowledge. Green's conception is barren for ethical purposes—it is merely an eternal intellect out of time.[1]

On the other hand, bearing in mind the influence of Aristotle upon Green,[2] and remembering the analysis of the psychological elements of moral action in *Proleg.* Book II., it might be thought that Green's ideal of human perfection, so far as ethical, belongs "rather to the human soul as a function of an animal organism, modified by being made a vehicle of the eternal consciousness, and not to that eternal consciousness itself, as making the animal organism the vehicle." We might infer that "it is only because it has supervened upon the appetitive life of an animal organism that the self-conscious self has such desires for the realisation of objects at all. And since the essential characteristic of moral action, as explained in Book II., consists in the presence of this self-distinguishing and self-seeking consciousness, identifying itself with different particular desires—or rather usually with a complex resultant of several distinguishable desires; I should have expected that man's pursuit of perfection would be traced to some combination of natural desires modified by self-consciousness."[3]

[1] *Mind*, p. 172.   [2] *Ibid.* p. 173.   [3] *Ibid.* p. 174.

"But the account of the moral ideal (in Book III.) does not correspond to this expectation; the impulse of the spirit to seek 'moral good' is rather represented as being in profound contrast and antagonism to the impulses of the animal soul . . , accordingly, though 'good' is defined as 'that which satisfies some desire,' 'moral good,' or the 'true good' is defined as 'an end in which the effort of a moral agent may really find *rest*,' or, as Green elsewhere expresses it, 'an abiding satisfaction of an abiding self.'"

In fact (to digress for a moment), Green's "only substantial objection to the Hedonistic end relates to its transient quality; it is not a permanent or abiding good."[1] This argument, with the accompanying paradox that a "greatest sum of pleasures is intrinsically unmeaning," need not be seriously refuted by the Hedonist. Happiness *in* life is made up of the continual fresh emergence of desire, and the consequent succession of particular pleasure or gratifications, and "rest" is neither desired nor attainable.

To return—the questions at once arise (1), What is this permanent or abiding good?[2]

(2) What ground have we for supposing it attainable by man?

The latter question is particularly apposite, for, in ordinary experience, the path of moral progress is

[1] *Mind*, p. 175. [2] *Ibid.* p. 177.

not one in which the effort of the moral agent finds "rest," and though Green says of the "man who calmly faces a life of suffering in the fulfilment of what he conceives to be his mission," that "*if* he could obtain the consciousness of having accomplished his work . . . he would find satisfaction in the consciousness," he adds, that "*probably just in proportion to the elevation of his character he is unable to do so.*"[1] Even if we admit the life after death, that gives us no ethical end here, and we ought not to use these theological notions as the basis of a philosophy of practice.

Leaving these difficulties, " can we find the 'abiding self-satisfaction' which a moral agent is supposed to seek . . . in the conception of a society of persons who somewhere, somehow, in the indefinite future, are to carry further that movement towards perfection which is so seriously impeded among the human beings whom we know?"[2] Possibly, if a "better state of humanity" could be taken as a convertible term for the "better state of myself" at which I, as a moral agent, necessarily aim. But can it? Green seems to use these two notions indifferently, but it is difficult to see " by what logical process we pass from the form of unqualified egoism, under which the true end of the moral agent is represented to us on one page, to the unmediated universalism which we find suddenly substituted for

[1] *Mind*, p. 177.   [2] *Ibid.* p. 179.

it on another.... The mere fact that I am aware of myself as a self-distinguishing consciousness, and attribute a similar consciousness to other men, does not necessarily make me regard their good as my own; some rational transition is still needed between the recognition of them as ends to themselves, and the recognition of them as ends to myself." Even if we assume "essential sociality of men, the universal or normal implication, through sympathy, of each one's interest or good with the interests of some others (as eighteenth-century optimism did), this only proves that I cannot realise good for myself without promoting the good of others in some degree; it does not show that my own good is in any sense identical with the good of others who are to live after me."[1] The majority of us may perhaps feel that our life, if not enlarged by sympathy, is meagre and starved, but this is far from constituting the good of humanity my good, and "it remains true that to most persons the dissatisfaction caused by the idea of the imperfection of other beings, not connected with them by some special bond of sympathy, is at any rate an evil very faintly perceptible; and the question why in this case they should sacrifice any material part of their own good or perfection to avoid it remains unanswered." So again the "habitual self-denial," the "self-sacrificing will," which form an essential element of Green's

[1] *Mind*, p. 181.

moral ideal, cannot be justified by his theory of the true good. We seem continually to find, in his account of moral action, pagan or neo-pagan forms of ethical thought combined with Christian or post-Christian forms, without any proper philosophical reconciliation.[1]

We are led into similar inconsistencies if we include (as Green does) artistic and scientific development, in addition to virtue proper, in the conception of the true good. Here Green seems to have unconsciously tried to get the advantages of two distinct and incompatible conceptions of human good; the one liberally comprehensive, but palpably admitting competition, the other non-competitive but stoically or puritanically narrow.[2]

If, finally, we look at the two criteria of moral action—the formal and the material—we find Green halting between two opinions which cannot be combined, except in a dogmatic and unjustifiable way. On the one hand, the one unconditional good is the "good will"; on the other, a man "cannot have been good unless he has done what is good in result." It is true that Green dogmatically enunciates that "there is no real reason to doubt that the good or evil in the motive of an action is exactly measured by the good or evil in its consequences as rightly estimated." "With the whole spiritual history of the action before us on the one side, with the whole

[1] *Mind*, p. 183.   [2] *Ibid.* p. 184.

sum and series of its effects before us on the other, we should presumably see that just so far as a good will . . . has had more or less to do with bringing the action about, there is more or less good . . . in its effects"; but nothing that can be called evidence is offered on behalf of this startling presumption.[1]

These difficulties prevent our finding in Green any consistent method by which a system of duties can be philosophically worked out. There is much instructive description and discussion, in the concluding book of the treatise, of the general attitude which a moral man should adopt in dealing with practical problems, much subtle analysis and distinction of different elements presented for his consideration; but if the reader expects to be guided to a cogently reasoned solution of any such problems—proceeding from unambiguous ethical premises to definite practical conclusions—the expectation will hardly be fulfilled.

§ 6. Speaking generally of the criticism above summarised, it may be said that if the positive theory underlying it (and from which all its force is really derived), as to the nature of man, were true, it would form a plausible attack upon Green's position. This underlying theory is that of Rational Hedonism, of which the main assumptions are (1) that happiness in life does consist in a series of particular pleasures; (2) that human society is an

[1] *Mind*, p. 185.

aggregate of particular individuals in this sense at least, that the "self-gratification" the individual members respectively pursue often involves a conflict of interests, so that one man's gain implies another's loss. From such a standpoint Green's "identification of the self and society" seems necessarily foolishness, and his belief that the "good of humanity is also my good" a gratuitous misconception. This raises really not an Ethical but a Metaphysical question, viz., "What is the nature of man?" Green's answer will be obvious from the earlier pages of this book, and to discuss here this difference between him and Professor Sidgwick would be out of place. Hedonism is not a criticism of Green, but a positive theory resting upon a metaphysical basis of its own, which is opposed antithetically to that of Green. To attack this theory directly is no part of our present task; to meet the objections based upon it, by re-establishing Green's metaphysical position would be to repeat what has been already said. Yet one or other of these alternative courses is the only satisfactory method of answering Professor Sidgwick's criticism.

If we, however, bear in mind that the real answer to Professor Sidgwick is contained in chapters ii. and iii. of this book, a few additional remarks upon the five points raised in his article will not be out of place.

It will be convenient to take them separately :—

(1) The conception of the Eternal Consciousness (in Book I.), and the perfection which the human spirit can attain as reproduction of such a consciousness, is purely intellectual, not moral. An "eternal intellect out of time is barren for ethical purposes."

The answer to this is that Book I. is purposely confined to the subject of "knowledge," to the exclusion of "virtue," but that its conclusions, so far from picturing man's perfection as "increase of knowledge," emphasise the truth that he, and he alone, is capable of *action*. We *must* ask first what the nature of man is, if our labour as Moralists is to be assured against being wasted labour. Book I. deals with this question, and finds that man is not only fitted for knowledge, but is also a "free cause"—in other words, is capable of action. In this way we advance, naturally, to consider what man has in him to become; for the moral world is a world which man creates for himself. He does not receive it as he receives the world of knowledge. Book I. shows the possibility of such a world, and so prepares the foundation upon which the later books build the detailed structure called the Moral Ideal. Taken abstractedly by itself, it is, doubtless, true to say that no Moral Ideal can be found in it; but such abstraction is not only unfair, it is unmeaning.

(2) Seeing that the good is defined as the conscious recognition (and satisfaction of) a desire, the true good, or Moral Ideal, ought to consist of "some combination of natural desires, modified by self-consciousness," whereas Green pictures the "impulse to moral good as being in profound contrast and antagonism to the impulses of the animal soul."

This objection seems partly to ignore the vital distinction Green draws (*Prolegomena*, Book II. ch. i.) between animal "want" and human "motive," partly to forget Green's emphatic warning not to confuse the conflicting impulses which affect the man "before he has made up his mind" with that "desire," in the satisfaction of which he realises his true Self. Man is not a sum of particular impulses, nor can any one of these, even if afterwards "chosen," be rightly, before the choice is made, be considered "his desire." Nor, again, is "the abiding satisfaction of the abiding self" a mere sum of particular pleasures—it is the formation of character, the gradual building-up of that "person" in which we recognise our "Moral Ideal" to consist. Professor Sidgwick's misunderstanding is so radical, that it can only be accounted for by remembering the assumption he starts with, viz., that happiness is unmeaning except as a sum of particular pleasures arising from the gratification of particular desires. A clear conception of what Green means by "desire," will leave no doubt as to the irrelevancy of any criticism which identifies such a sum of pleasures with the "self-satisfaction" of the *Prolegomena*. The divergence of view is, in fact, paradoxically, but unmistakably, brought out by Green himself in the words (*v. Prolegomena*, 171), "Whereas with them" (*i.e.* the Hedonists) "the good generically is the pleasant; in this treatise the common characteristic of the good is that it satisfies some desire."

(3) The point of the third objection lies in the question, "Why should I recognise other men's good as my own?" or, expressed a little differently, "Why should I sacrifice my good to that of others?"

The answer is—Because they are not "other." A society (so-called) in which the individuals composing it can only get their own good each at the expense of some one else—a society, in other words, of atomic units—is not a human society at all. It may possibly represent a stage—animal or barbarian—through which we have, as historical fact, passed; but it is unmeaning now. To the infant, if we could imagine him aware of himself and his wants, other people might, perhaps, appear as "other," and the fundamental rule of conduct be represented by "each for himself," but with every upward step of the intellectual ladder, as he grows into manhood, he comes to see that the

"Self," in concrete actuality, is literally made up of other selves, and that (to put the matter practically) to refuse to fulfil obligations binding upon him *quâ* father, tutor, fellow-soldier, &c., &c., is simply to commit suicide. Happiness is not a "moral plum-cake which won't go quite round"; it is something attainable only in the discharge of function, and a man's function is to be in actuality that part of the social organism he recognises himself to be. Without this recognition man is not even a man; with it, the obligation to "sacrifice myself for others" is self-evident.

(4) Similar inconsistencies arise if we include (as Green does) artistic and scientific development, in addition to virtue proper, in the conception of the true good.

To this statement of Professor Sidgwick no definite answer is possible, because we have not sufficient data to go upon. Green raises the question in *Prolegomena*, § 289, but does not discuss it, explaining (§ 290) that "it shall be dealt with in the sequel, and is noticed here in order to record the writer's admission that it cannot be passed over."

Upon this an editorial footnote runs as follows: "The question is not discussed in the *Prolegomena to Ethics*, and from a mark at this point in the author's MS., it is almost certain that he had abandoned the idea of dealing with it in the present volume. . . . The reader will probably gather from Book III. a general idea of the way in which the difficulty would have been met, especially if he remembers that the end has been throughout defined as the realisation of the possibilities of human nature; and that devotion to such objects as the well-being of a family, the sanitation of a town, or the composition of a book, has been described as an unconscious pursuit of this end. . . ."

It is tempting, assuredly, to hold a brief for Green *v.* Sidgwick; but in dealing with a criticism which professedly confines itself to the *Prolegomena*, it is impossible to overstep the same limits.

(5) Lastly, Professor Sidgwick complains of the want of practical value—"there is much instructive description and discussion of the general attitude which a moral man should adopt in dealing with practical problems . . . but there is no cogently-reasoned solution of any such problems, proceeding from unambiguous ethical premises to definite practical conclusions."

The accusation is true, but perhaps not exactly fair. The *Prolegomena to Ethics* is a philosophical enquiry into the nature of man, in order to find in what his true good ultimately consists. It does not profess to be a treatise on casuistry, still less does it try to discharge the function of a "moral ready-reckoner." The practical value of moral theory, while very real, Green holds to be " rather negative than positive";[1] and the philosopher is of most use when confining himself to his proper task. "It may ... fall to the moral philosopher, under certain conditions of society and of intellectual movement, to render an important practical service. But he will render it simply by fulfilling with the utmost possible completeness his proper work of analysis. As a *moral* philosopher, he analyses human conduct, the motives which it expresses, the spiritual endowments implied in it, the history of thought, habits, and institutions through which it has come to be what it is. He does not understand his business as a philosopher, if he claims to do more than this."[2] He is of practical use "by giving the most adequate account possible of the moral ideal; by considering the process through which the institutions and rules of life, of which we acknowledge the authority, have arisen out of the effort, however blindly directed, after such an ideal, and have in their several measures contributed to its realisation; by showing that conscience in the individual, while owing its education to those institutions and rules, is not properly the mere organ of any or all of them, but may freely and in its own right apprehend the ideal, of which they are more or less inadequate expressions; by thus doing his proper work as a philosopher of morals, he may help the soul to rise above the region of distraction between competing authorities,

[1] *Cf. Proleg.* § 311.   [2] *Proleg.* § 327.

or between authorities and an inner law, to a region in which it can harmonise all the authorities by looking to the end to which they, or whatever is really authoritative in them, no less than the inner law, are alike relative."[1]

[1] *Proleg.* § 327.

PLYMOUTH
WILLIAM BRENDON AND SON
PRINTERS

A SELECTION OF BOOKS PUBLISHED BY METHUEN AND CO. LTD., LONDON
36 ESSEX STREET
W.C.

CONTENTS

	PAGE		PAGE
General Literature	2	Little Quarto Shakespeare	19
Ancient Cities	12	Miniature Library	19
Antiquary's Books	13	New Library of Medicine	19
Arden Shakespeare	13	New Library of Music	20
Classics of Art	14	Oxford Biographies	20
Complete Series	14	Romantic History	20
Connoisseur's Library	14	States of Italy	20
Handbooks of English Church History	15	Westminster Commentaries	21
Handbooks of Theology	15	Shilling Library	21
Illustrated Pocket Library of Plain and Coloured Books	15	Fiction	21
Leaders of Religion	16	Two-Shilling Novels	26
Library of Devotion	16	Books for Boys and Girls	26
Little Books on Art	17	Shilling Novels	26
Little Galleries	17	Novels of Alexandre Dumas	27
Little Guides	17	Sixpenny Books	27
Little Library	18	Books for Travellers	30
		Some Books on Art	30
		Some Books on Italy	31

MARCH 1912

A SELECTION OF

MESSRS. METHUEN'S

PUBLICATIONS

In this Catalogue the order is according to authors. An asterisk denotes that the book is in the press.

Colonial Editions are published of all Messrs. METHUEN'S Novels issued at a price above 2s. 6d., and similar editions are published of some works of General Literature. Colonial editions are only for circulation in the British Colonies and India.

All books marked net are not subject to discount, and cannot be bought at less than the published price. Books not marked net are subject to the discount which the bookseller allows.

Messrs. METHUEN'S books are kept in stock by all good booksellers. If there is any difficulty in seeing copies, Messrs. Methuen will be very glad to have early information, and specimen copies of any books will be sent on receipt of the published price *plus* postage for net books, and of the published price for ordinary books.

This Catalogue contains only a selection of the more important books published by Messrs. Methuen. A complete and illustrated catalogue of their publications may be obtained on application.

Andrewes (Lancelot). PRECES PRIVATAE. Translated and edited, with Notes, by F. E. BRIGHTMAN. *Cr. 8vo.* 6s.

Aristotle. THE ETHICS. Edited, with an Introduction and Notes, by JOHN BURNET. *Demy 8vo.* 10s. 6d. net.

Atkinson (C. T.). A HISTORY OF GERMANY, from 1715-1815. Illustrated. *Demy 8vo.* 12s. 6d. net.

Atkinson (T. D.). ENGLISH ARCHITECTURE. Illustrated. *Fcap. 8vo.* 3s. 6d. net.
A GLOSSARY OF TERMS USED IN ENGLISH ARCHITECTURE. Illustrated. *Second Edition. Fcap. 8vo.* 3s. 6d. net.

Bain (F. W.). A DIGIT OF THE MOON: A HINDOO LOVE STORY. *Ninth Edition. Fcap. 8vo.* 3s. 6d. net.
THE DESCENT OF THE SUN: A CYCLE OF BIRTH. *Fifth Edition. Fcap. 8vo.* 3s. 6d. net.
A HEIFER OF THE DAWN. *Seventh Edition. Fcap. 8vo.* 2s. 6d. net.
IN THE GREAT GOD'S HAIR. *Fifth Edition. Fcap. 8vo.* 2s. 6d. net.
A DRAUGHT OF THE BLUE. *Fourth Edition. Fcap. 8vo.* 2s. 6d. net.
AN ESSENCE OF THE DUSK. *Third Edition. Fcap. 8vo.* 2s. 6d. net.
AN INCARNATION OF THE SNOW. *Second Edition. Fcap. 8vo.* 3s. 6d. net.
A MINE OF FAULTS. *Second Edition. Fcap. 8vo.* 3s. 6d. net.
THE ASHES OF A GOD. *Fcap. 8vo.* 3s. 6d. net.

Balfour (Graham). THE LIFE OF ROBERT LOUIS STEVENSON. Illustrated. *Fifth Edition in one Volume. Cr. 8vo. Buckram,* 6s.

Baring-Gould (S.). THE LIFE OF NAPOLEON BONAPARTE. Illustrated. *Second Edition. Royal 8vo.* 10s. 6d. net.
THE TRAGEDY OF THE CÆSARS: A STUDY OF THE CHARACTERS OF THE CÆSARS OF THE JULIAN AND CLAUDIAN HOUSES. Illustrated. *Seventh Edition. Royal 8vo.* 10s. 6d. net.
A BOOK OF FAIRY TALES. Illustrated. *Second Edition. Cr. 8vo.* 6s. Also *Medium 8vo.* 6d.
OLD ENGLISH FAIRY TALES. Illustrated. *Third Edition. Cr. 8vo. Buckram.* 6s.
THE VICAR OF MORWENSTOW. With a Portrait. *Third Edition. Cr. 8vo.* 3s. 6d.
OLD COUNTRY LIFE. Illustrated. *Fifth Edition. Large Cr. 8vo.* 6s.
STRANGE SURVIVALS: SOME CHAPTERS IN THE HISTORY OF MAN. Illustrated. *Third Edition. Cr. 8vo.* 2s. 6d. net.

YORKSHIRE ODDITIES: INCIDENTS AND STRANGE EVENTS. *Fifth Edition. Cr. 8vo.* 2s. 6d. net.
A BOOK OF CORNWALL. Illustrated. *Third Edition. Cr. 8vo.* 6s.
A BOOK OF DARTMOOR. Illustrated. *Second Edition. Cr. 8vo.* 6s.
A BOOK OF DEVON. Illustrated. *Third Edition. Cr. 8vo.* 6s.
A BOOK OF NORTH WALES. Illustrated. *Cr. 8vo.* 6s.
A BOOK OF SOUTH WALES. Illustrated. *Cr. 8vo.* 6s.
A BOOK OF BRITTANY. Illustrated. *Second Edition. Cr. 8vo.* 6s.
A BOOK OF THE RHINE: From Cleve to Mainz. Illustrated. *Second Edition. Cr. 8vo.* 6s.
A BOOK OF THE RIVIERA. Illustrated. *Second Edition. Cr. 8vo.* 6s.
A BOOK OF THE PYRENEES. Illustrated. *Cr. 8vo.* 6s.

Baring-Gould (S.) and Sheppard (H. Fleetwood). A GARLAND OF COUNTRY SONG. English Folk Songs with their Traditional Melodies. *Demy 4to.* 6s.
SONGS OF THE WEST: Folk Songs of Devon and Cornwall. Collected from the Mouths of the People. New and Revised Edition, under the musical editorship of CECIL J. SHARP. *Large Imperial 8vo.* 5s. net.

Barker (E.). THE POLITICAL THOUGHT OF PLATO AND ARISTOTLE. *Demy 8vo.* 10s. 6d. net.

Bastable (C. F.). THE COMMERCE OF NATIONS. *Fifth Edition. Cr. 8vo.* 2s. 6d.

Batson (Mrs. Stephen). A CONCISE HANDBOOK OF GARDEN FLOWERS. *Fcap. 8vo.* 3s. 6d.

Beckett (Arthur). THE SPIRIT OF THE DOWNS: Impressions and Reminiscences of the Sussex Downs. Illustrated. *Second Edition. Demy 8vo.* 10s. 6d. net.

Beckford (Peter). THOUGHTS ON HUNTING. Edited by J. OTHO PAGET. Illustrated. *Third Edition. Demy 8vo.* 6s.

Belloc (H.). PARIS. Illustrated. *Second Edition, Revised. Cr. 8vo.* 6s.
HILLS AND THE SEA. *Fourth Edition. Fcap. 8vo.* 5s.
ON NOTHING AND KINDRED SUBJECTS. *Third Edition. Fcap. 8vo.* 5s.
ON EVERYTHING. *Third Edition. Fcap. 8vo.* 5s.
ON SOMETHING. *Second Edition. Fcap. 8vo.* 5s.
FIRST AND LAST. *Fcap. 8vo.* 5s.
MARIE ANTOINETTE. Illustrated. *Third Edition. Demy 8vo.* 15s. net.
THE PYRENEES. Illustrated. *Second Edition. Demy 8vo.* 7s. 6d. net.

Bennett (Arnold). THE HONEYMOON. *Second Edition. Fcap. 8vo.* 2s. net.

Bennett (W. H.). A PRIMER OF THE BIBLE. *Fifth Edition. Cr. 8vo.* 2s. 6d.

Bennett (W. H.) and Adeney (W. F.). A BIBLICAL INTRODUCTION. With a concise Bibliography. *Sixth Edition. Cr. 8vo.* 7s. 6d.

Benson (Archbishop). GOD'S BOARD. Communion Addresses. *Second Edition. Fcap. 8vo.* 3s. 6d. net.

Bensusan (Samuel L.). HOME LIFE IN SPAIN. Illustrated. *Second Edition. Demy 8vo.* 10s. 6d. net.

Betham-Edwards (Miss). HOME LIFE IN FRANCE. Illustrated. *Fifth Edition. Cr. 8vo.* 6s.

Bindley (T. Herbert). THE OECUMENICAL DOCUMENTS OF THE FAITH. With Introductions and Notes. *Second Edition. Cr. 8vo.* 6s. net.

Blake (William). ILLUSTRATIONS OF THE BOOK OF JOB. With a General Introduction by LAURENCE BINYON. Illustrated. *Quarto.* 21s. net.

Bloemfontein (Bishop of). ARA CŒLI: AN ESSAY IN MYSTICAL THEOLOGY. *Fourth Edition. Cr. 8vo.* 3s. 6d. net.
FAITH AND EXPERIENCE. *Second Edition. Cr. 8vo.* 3s. 6d. net.

Bowden (E. M.). THE IMITATION OF BUDDHA: Quotations from Buddhist Literature for each Day in the Year. *Sixth Edition. Cr. 16mo.* 2s. 6d.

Brabant (F. G.). RAMBLES IN SUSSEX. Illustrated. *Cr. 8vo.* 6s.

Bradley (A. G.). ROUND ABOUT WILTSHIRE. Illustrated. *Second Edition. Cr. 8vo.* 6s.
THE ROMANCE OF NORTHUMBERLAND. Illustrated. *Second Edition. Demy 8vo.* 7s. 6d. net.

Braid (James). ADVANCED GOLF. Illustrated. *Sixth Edition. Demy 8vo.* 10s. 6d. net.

Brailsford (H. N.). MACEDONIA: ITS RACES AND THEIR FUTURE. Illustrated. *Demy 8vo.* 12s. 6d. net.

Brodrick (Mary) and Morton (A. Anderson). A CONCISE DICTIONARY OF EGYPTIAN ARCHÆOLOGY. A Handbook for Students and Travellers. Illustrated. *Cr. 8vo.* 3s. 6d.

Browning (Robert). PARACELSUS. Edited with an Introduction, Notes, and Bibliography by MARGARET L. LEE and KATHARINE B. LOCOCK. *Fcap. 8vo.* 3s. 6d. net.

Buckton (A. M.). EAGER HEART: A Christmas Mystery-Play. *Tenth Edition.* *Cr. 8vo.* 1s. net.

Budge (E. A. Wallis). THE GODS OF THE EGYPTIANS. Illustrated. *Two Volumes. Royal 8vo.* £3 3s. net.

Bull (Paul). GOD AND OUR SOLDIERS. *Second Edition. Cr. 8vo.* 6s.

Burns (Robert). THE POEMS AND SONGS. Edited by ANDREW LANG and W. A. CRAIGIE. With Portrait. *Third Edition. Wide Demy 8vo.* 6s.

Busbey (Katherine G.). HOME LIFE IN AMERICA. Illustrated. *Second Edition. Demy 8vo.* 10s. 6d. net.

Butlin (F. M.). AMONG THE DANES. Illustrated. *Demy 8vo.* 7s. 6d. net.

Cain (Georges). WALKS IN PARIS. Translated by A. R. ALLINSON. Illustrated. *Demy 8vo.* 7s. 6d. net.

Calman (W. T.). THE LIFE OF CRUSTACEA. Illustrated. *Cr. 8vo.* 6s.

Carlyle (Thomas). THE FRENCH REVOLUTION. Edited by C. R. L. FLETCHER. *Three Volumes. Cr. 8vo.* 18s.
THE LETTERS AND SPEECHES OF OLIVER CROMWELL. With an Introduction by C. H. FIRTH, and Notes and Appendices by S. C. LOMAS. *Three Volumes. Demy 8vo.* 18s. net.

Celano (Brother Thomas of). THE LIVES OF S. FRANCIS OF ASSISI. Translated by A. G. FERRERS HOWELL. Illustrated. *Cr. 8vo.* 5s. net.

Chambers (Mrs. Lambert). LAWN TENNIS FOR LADIES. Illustrated. *Cr. 8vo.* 2s. 6d. net.

Chesterfield (Lord). THE LETTERS OF THE EARL OF CHESTERFIELD TO HIS SON. Edited, with an Introduction by C. STRACHEY, and Notes by A. CALTHROP. *Two Volumes. Cr. 8vo.* 12s.

Chesterton (G.K.). CHARLES DICKENS. With two Portraits in Photogravure. *Seventh Edition. Cr. 8vo.* 6s.
ALL THINGS CONSIDERED. *Sixth Edition. Fcap. 8vo.* 5s.
TREMENDOUS TRIFLES. *Fourth Edition. Fcap. 8vo.* 5s.
ALARMS AND DISCURSIONS. *Second Edition. Fcap. 8vo.* 5s.
THE BALLAD OF THE WHITE HORSE. *Third Edition. Fcap. 8vo.* 5s.

Clausen (George). SIX LECTURES ON PAINTING. Illustrated. *Third Edition. Large Post 8vo.* 3s. 6d. net.
AIMS AND IDEALS IN ART. Eight Lectures delivered to the Students of the Royal Academy of Arts. Illustrated. *Second Edition. Large Post 8vo.* 5s. net.

Clutton-Brock (A.) SHELLEY: THE MAN AND THE POET. Illustrated. *Demy 8vo.* 7s. 6d. net.

Cobb (W.F.). THE BOOK OF PSALMS: with an Introduction and Notes. *Demy 8vo.* 10s. 6d. net.

Collingwood (W. G.). THE LIFE OF JOHN RUSKIN. With Portrait. *Sixth Edition. Cr. 8vo.* 2s. 6d. net.

Conrad (Joseph). THE MIRROR OF THE SEA: Memories and Impressions. *Third Edition. Cr. 8vo.* 6s.

Coolidge (W. A. B.). THE ALPS. Illustrated. *Demy 8vo.* 7s. 6d. net.

Coulton (G. G.). CHAUCER AND HIS ENGLAND. Illustrated. *Second Edition. Demy 8vo.* 10s. 6d. net.

Cowper (William). THE POEMS. Edited with an Introduction and Notes by J. C. BAILEY. Illustrated. *Demy 8vo.* 10s. 6d. net.

Crispe (T. E.). REMINISCENCES OF A K.C. With 2 Portraits. *Second Edition. Demy 8vo.* 10s. 6d. net.

Crowley (Ralph H.). THE HYGIENE OF SCHOOL LIFE. Illustrated. *Cr. 8vo.* 3s. 6d. net.

Dante Alighieri. LA COMMEDIA DI DANTE. The Italian Text edited by PAGET TOYNBEE. *Cr. 8vo.* 6s.

Davey (Richard). THE PAGEANT OF LONDON. Illustrated. *In Two Volumes. Demy 8vo.* 15s. net.

Davis (H. W. C.). ENGLAND UNDER THE NORMANS AND ANGEVINS: 1066-1272. Illustrated. *Second Edition. Demy 8vo.* 10s. 6d. net.

Dawbarn (Charles.) FRANCE AND THE FRENCH. Illustrated. *Demy 8vo.* 10s. 6d. net.

Dearmer (Mabel). A CHILD'S LIFE OF CHRIST. Illustrated. *Large Cr. 8vo.* 6s.

Deffand (Madame Du). THE LETTERS OF MADAME DU DEFFAND TO HORACE WALPOLE. Edited, with Introduction, Notes, and Index, by Mrs. PAGET TOYNBEE. *In Three Volumes. Demy 8vo.* £3 3s. net.

Dickinson (G. L.). THE GREEK VIEW OF LIFE. *Seventh Edition. Crown 8vo.* 2s. 6d. net.

Ditchfield (P. H.). THE PARISH CLERK. Illustrated. *Third Edition. Demy 8vo.* 7s. 6d. net.
THE OLD-TIME PARSON. Illustrated. *Second Edition. Demy 8vo.* 7s. 6d. net.

General Literature

Ditchfield (P. H.) and Roe (Fred). VANISHING ENGLAND. The Book by P. H. Ditchfield. Illustrated by FRED ROE. *Second Edition. Wide Demy 8vo.* 15s. net.

Douglas (Hugh A.). VENICE ON FOOT. With the Itinerary of the Grand Canal. Illustrated. *Second Edition. Fcap. 8vo.* 5s. net.
VENICE AND HER TREASURES. Illustrated. *Round corners. Fcap. 8vo.* 5s. net.

Dowden (J.). FURTHER STUDIES IN THE PRAYER BOOK. *Cr. 8vo.* 6s.

Driver (S. R.). SERMONS ON SUBJECTS CONNECTED WITH THE OLD TESTAMENT. *Cr. 8vo.* 6s.

Dumas (Alexandre). THE CRIMES OF THE BORGIAS AND OTHERS. With an Introduction by R. S. GARNETT. Illustrated. *Second Edition. Cr. 8vo.* 6s.
THE CRIMES OF URBAIN GRANDIER AND OTHERS. Illustrated. *Cr. 8vo.* 6s.
THE CRIMES OF THE MARQUISE DE BRINVILLIERS AND OTHERS. Illustrated. *Cr. 8vo.* 6s.
THE CRIMES OF ALI PACHA AND OTHERS. Illustrated. *Cr. 8vo.* 6s.
MY MEMOIRS. Translated by E. M. WALLER. With an Introduction by ANDREW LANG. With Frontispieces in Photogravure. In six Volumes. *Cr. 8vo.* 6s. each volume.
VOL. I. 1802-1821. VOL. IV. 1830-1831.
VOL. II. 1822-1825. VOL. V. 1831-1832.
VOL. III. 1826-1830. VOL. VI. 1832-1833.
MY PETS. Newly translated by A. R. ALLINSON. Illustrated. *Cr. 8vo.* 6s.

Duncan (F. M.). OUR INSECT FRIENDS AND FOES. Illustrated. *Cr. 8vo.* 6s.

Dunn-Pattison (R. P.). NAPOLEON'S MARSHALS. Illustrated. *Demy 8vo. Second Edition.* 12s. 6d. net.
THE BLACK PRINCE. Illustrated. *Second Edition. Demy 8vo.* 7s. 6d. net.

Durham (The Earl of). THE REPORT ON CANADA. With an Introductory Note. *Demy 8vo.* 4s. 6d. net.

Dutt (W. A.). THE NORFOLK BROADS. Illustrated. *Second Edition. Cr. 8vo.* 6s.
WILD LIFE IN EAST ANGLIA. Illustrated. *Second Edition. Demy 8vo.* 7s. 6d. net.

Edwardes (Tickner). THE LORE OF THE HONEY-BEE. Illustrated. *Third Edition. Cr. 8vo.* 6s.
LIFT-LUCK ON SOUTHERN ROADS. Illustrated. *Cr. 8vo.* 6s.
NEIGHBOURHOOD: A YEAR'S LIFE IN AND ABOUT AN ENGLISH VILLAGE. Illustrated. *Cr. 8vo.* 6s.

Egerton (H. E.). A SHORT HISTORY OF BRITISH COLONIAL POLICY. *Third Edition. Demy 8vo.* 7s. 6d. net.

Exeter (Bishop of). REGNUM DEI. (The Bampton Lectures of 1901.) *A Cheaper Edition. Demy 8vo.* 7s. 6d. net.

Fairbrother (W. H.). THE PHILOSOPHY OF T. H. GREEN. *Second Edition. Cr. 8vo.* 3s. 6d.

Fea (Allan). THE FLIGHT OF THE KING. Illustrated. *Second and Revised Edition. Demy 8vo.* 7s. 6d. net.
SECRET CHAMBERS AND HIDING-PLACES. Illustrated. *Third and Revised Edition. Demy 8vo.* 7s. 6d. net.
JAMES II. AND HIS WIVES. Illustrated. *Demy 8vo.* 12s. 6d. net.

Firth (C. H.). CROMWELL'S ARMY: A History of the English Soldier during the Civil Wars, the Commonwealth, and the Protectorate. Illustrated. *Second Edition. Cr. 8vo.* 6s.

Fisher (H. A. L.). THE REPUBLICAN TRADITION IN EUROPE. *Cr. 8vo.* 6s. net.

FitzGerald (Edward). THE RUBAI'YAT OF OMAR KHAYYÁM. Printed from the Fifth and last Edition. With a Commentary by H. M. BATSON, and a Biographical Introduction by E. D. ROSS. *Cr. 8vo.* 6s.

Fletcher (J. S.). A BOOK ABOUT YORKSHIRE. Illustrated. *Demy 8vo.* 7s. 6d. net.

Flux (A. W.). ECONOMIC PRINCIPLES. *Demy 8vo.* 7s. 6d. net.

Fraser (J. F.). ROUND THE WORLD ON A WHEEL. Illustrated. *Fifth Edition. Cr. 8vo.* 6s.

Galton (Sir Francis). MEMORIES OF MY LIFE. Illustrated. *Third Edition. Demy 8vo.* 10s. 6d. net.

Gibbins (H. de B.). INDUSTRY IN ENGLAND: HISTORICAL OUTLINES. With 5 Maps. *Sixth Edition. Demy 8vo.* 10s. 6d.
THE INDUSTRIAL HISTORY OF ENGLAND. Illustrated. *Eighteenth and Revised Edition. Cr. 8vo.* 3s.
ENGLISH SOCIAL REFORMERS. *Second Edition. Cr. 8vo.* 2s. 6d.

Gibbon (Edward). THE MEMOIRS OF THE LIFE OF EDWARD GIBBON. Edited by G. BIRKBECK HILL. *Cr. 8vo.* 6s.
THE DECLINE AND FALL OF THE ROMAN EMPIRE. Edited, with Notes, Appendices, and Maps, by J. B. BURY, Illustrated. *In Seven Volumes. Demy 8vo.* Each 10s. 6d. net.

Gloag (M. R.) A BOOK OF ENGLISH GARDENS. Illustrated. *Demy 8vo. 10s. 6d. net.*

Glover (J. M.). JIMMY GLOVER—HIS BOOK. *Fourth Edition. Demy 8vo. 12s. 6d. net.*

Glover (T. R.). THE CONFLICT OF RELIGIONS IN THE EARLY ROMAN EMPIRE. *Fourth Edition. Demy 8vo. 7s. 6d. net.*

Godfrey (Elizabeth). A BOOK OF REMEMBRANCE. Being Lyrical Selections for every day in the Year. Arranged by E. Godfrey. *Second Edition. Fcap. 8vo. 2s. 6d. net.*

Godley (A. D.). OXFORD IN THE EIGHTEENTH CENTURY. Illustrated. *Second Edition. Demy 8vo. 7s. 6d. net.*
LYRA FRIVOLA. *Fourth Edition. Fcap. 8vo. 2s. 6d.*
VERSES TO ORDER. *Second Edition. Fcap. 8vo. 2s. 6d.*
SECOND STRINGS. *Fcap. 8vo. 2s. 6d.*

Gordon (Lina Duff) (Mrs. Aubrey Waterfield). HOME LIFE IN ITALY: LETTERS FROM THE APENNINES. Illustrated. *Second Edition. Demy 8vo. 10s. 6d. net.*

Gostling (Frances M.). THE BRETONS AT HOME. Illustrated. *Third Edition. Cr. 8vo. 6s.*
AUVERGNE AND ITS PEOPLE. Illustrated. *Demy 8vo. 10s. 6d. net.*

Grahame (Kenneth). THE WIND IN THE WILLOWS. Illustrated. *Sixth Edition. Cr. 8vo. 6s.*

Grew (Edwin Sharpe). THE GROWTH OF A PLANET. Illustrated. *Cr. 8vo. 6s.*

Griffin (W. Hall) and **Minchin (H. C.).** THE LIFE OF ROBERT BROWNING. Illustrated. *Second Edition. Demy 8vo. 12s. 6d. net.*

Hale (J. R.). FAMOUS SEA FIGHTS: FROM SALAMIS TO TSU-SHIMA. Illustrated. *Cr. 8vo. 6s. net.*

Hall (Cyril). THE YOUNG CARPENTER. Illustrated. *Cr. 8vo. 5s.*

Hall (Hammond). THE YOUNG ENGINEER; or MODERN ENGINES AND THEIR MODELS. Illustrated. *Second Edition. Cr. 8vo. 5s.*
THE YOUNG ELECTRICIAN. Illustrated. *Second Edition. Cr. 8vo. 5s.*

Hannay (D.). A SHORT HISTORY OF THE ROYAL NAVY. Vol. I., 1217-1688. Vol. II., 1689-1815. *Demy 8vo. Each 7s. 6d. net.*

Harper (Charles G.). THE AUTOCAR ROAD-BOOK. Four Volumes with Maps. *Cr. 8vo. Each 7s. 6d. net.*
Vol. I.—SOUTH OF THE THAMES.
Vol. II.—NORTH AND SOUTH WALES AND WEST MIDLANDS.

Hassall (Arthur). NAPOLEON. Illustrated. *Demy 8vo. 7s. 6d. net.*

Headley (F. W.). DARWINISM AND MODERN SOCIALISM. *Second Edition. Cr. 8vo. 5s. net.*

Henderson (B. W.). THE LIFE AND PRINCIPATE OF THE EMPEROR NERO. Illustrated. *New and cheaper issue. Demy 8vo. 7s. 6d. net.*

Henderson (M. Sturge). GEORGE MEREDITH: NOVELIST, POET, REFORMER. Illustrated. *Second Edition. Cr. 8vo. 6s.*

Henderson (T. F.) and **Watt (Francis).** SCOTLAND OF TO-DAY. Illustrated. *Second Edition. Cr. 8vo. 6s.*

Henley (W. E.). ENGLISH LYRICS. CHAUCER TO POE. *Second Edition. Cr. 8vo. 2s. 6d. net.*

Hill (George Francis). ONE HUNDRED MASTERPIECES OF SCULPTURE. Illustrated. *Demy 8vo. 10s. 6d. net.*

Hind (C. Lewis). DAYS IN CORNWALL. Illustrated. *Third Edition. Cr. 8vo. 6s.*

Hobhouse (L. T.). THE THEORY OF KNOWLEDGE. *Demy 8vo. 10s. 6d. net.*

Hodgson (Mrs. W.). HOW TO IDENTIFY OLD CHINESE PORCELAIN. Illustrated. *Third Edition. Post 8vo. 6s.*

Holdich (Sir T. H.). THE INDIAN BORDERLAND, 1880-1900. Illustrated. *Second Edition. Demy 8vo. 10s. 6d. net.*

Holdsworth (W. S.). A HISTORY OF ENGLISH LAW. *In Four Volumes. Vols. I., II., III. Demy 8vo. Each 10s. 6d. net.*

Holland (Clive). TYROL AND ITS PEOPLE. Illustrated. *Demy 8vo. 10s. 6d. net.*
THE BELGIANS AT HOME. Illustrated. *Demy 8vo. 10s. 6d. net.*

Horsburgh (E. L. S.). LORENZO THE MAGNIFICENT: AND FLORENCE IN HER GOLDEN AGE. Illustrated. *Second Edition. Demy 8vo. 15s. net.*
WATERLOO: A NARRATIVE AND A CRITICISM. With Plans. *Second Edition. Cr. 8vo. 5s.*
THE LIFE OF SAVONAROLA. Illustrated. *Cr. 8vo. 5s. net.*

Hosie (Alexander). MANCHURIA. Illustrated. *Second Edition. Demy 8vo. 7s. 6d. net.*

Hudson (W. H.). A SHEPHERD'S LIFE: IMPRESSIONS OF THE SOUTH WILTSHIRE DOWNS. Illustrated. *Third Edition. Demy 8vo. 7s. 6d. net.*

General Literature

Hugon (Cécile). SOCIAL LIFE IN FRANCE IN THE XVII. CENTURY. Illustrated. *Demy 8vo.* 10s. 6d. *net*.

Humphreys (John H.). PROPORTIONAL REPRESENTATION. *Cr. 8vo.* 5s. *net*.

Hutchinson (Horace G.). THE NEW FOREST. Illustrated. *Fourth Edition. Cr. 8vo.* 6s.

Hutton (Edward). THE CITIES OF SPAIN. Illustrated. *Fourth Edition. Cr. 8vo.* 6s.
THE CITIES OF UMBRIA. Illustrated. *Fourth Edition. Cr. 8vo.* 6s.
FLORENCE AND THE CITIES OF NORTHERN TUSCANY WITH GENOA. Illustrated. *Second Edition. Cr. 8vo.* 6s.
SIENA AND SOUTHERN TUSCANY. Illustrated. *Second Edition. Cr. 8vo.* 6s.
VENICE AND VENETIA. Illustrated. *Cr. 8vo.* 6s.
ROME. Illustrated. *Second Edition. Cr. 8vo.* 6s.
ENGLISH LOVE POEMS. Edited with an Introduction. *Fcap. 8vo.* 3s. 6d. *net*.
COUNTRY WALKS ABOUT FLORENCE. Illustrated. *Second Edition. Fcap. 8vo.* 5s. *net*.
IN UNKNOWN TUSCANY With Notes by WILLIAM HEYWOOD. Illustrated. *Second Edition. Demy 8vo.* 7s. 6d. *net*.
A BOOK OF THE WYE. Illustrated. *Demy 8vo.* 7s. 6d. *net*.

Ibsen (Henrik). BRAND. A Dramatic Poem, Translated by WILLIAM WILSON. *Fourth Edition. Cr. 8vo.* 3s. 6d.

Inge (W. R.). CHRISTIAN MYSTICISM. (The Bampton Lectures of 1899.) *Second and Cheaper Edition. Cr. 8vo.* 5s. *net*.

Innes (A. D.). A HISTORY OF THE BRITISH IN INDIA. With Maps and Plans. *Cr. 8vo.* 6s.
ENGLAND UNDER THE TUDORS. With Maps. *Third Edition. Demy 8vo.* 10s. 6d. *net*.

Innes (Mary). SCHOOLS OF PAINTING. Illustrated. *Second Edition. Cr. 8vo.* 5s. *net*.

Jenks (E.). AN OUTLINE OF ENGLISH LOCAL GOVERNMENT. *Second Edition.* Revised by R. C. K. ENSOR. *Cr. 8vo.* 2s. 6d. *net*.

Jerningham (Charles Edward). THE MAXIMS OF MARMADUKE. *Second Edition. Cr. 8vo.* 5s.

Jerrold (Walter). THE DANUBE. Illustrated. *Demy 8vo.* 10s. 6d. *net*.

Johnston (Sir H. H.). BRITISH CENTRAL AFRICA. Illustrated. *Third Edition. Cr. 4to.* 18s. *net*.
THE NEGRO IN THE NEW WORLD. Illustrated. *Demy 8vo.* 21s. *net*.

Julian (Lady) of Norwich. REVELATIONS OF DIVINE LOVE. Edited by GRACE WARRACK. *Fourth Edition. Cr. 8vo.* 3s. 6d.

Keats (John). THE POEMS. Edited with Introduction and Notes by E. de SÉLINCOURT. With a Frontispiece in Photogravure. *Third Edition. Demy 8vo.* 7s. 6d. *net*.

Keble (John). THE CHRISTIAN YEAR. With an Introduction and Notes by W. LOCK. Illustrated. *Third Edition. Fcap. 8vo.* 3s. 6d.

Kempis (Thomas à). THE IMITATION OF CHRIST. With an Introduction by DEAN FARRAR. Illustrated. *Third Edition. Fcap. 8vo.* 3s. 6d.; *padded morocco*, 5s.

Kipling (Rudyard). BARRACK-ROOM BALLADS. 105th Thousand. *Thirtieth Edition. Cr. 8vo.* 6s. Also *Fcap. 8vo*, *Leather*. 5s. *net*.
THE SEVEN SEAS. 86th Thousand. *Eighteenth Edition. Cr. 8vo.* 6s. Also *Fcap. 8vo, Leather*. 5s. *net*.
THE FIVE NATIONS. 72nd Thousand. *Eighth Edition. Cr. 8vo.* 6s. Also *Fcap. 8vo, Leather*. 5s. *net*.
DEPARTMENTAL DITTIES. *Twentieth Edition. Cr. 8vo.* 6s. Also *Fcap. 8vo, Leather*. 5s. *net*.

Knox (Winifred F.). THE COURT OF A SAINT. Illustrated. *Demy 8vo.* 10s. 6d. *net*.

***Lamb (Charles and Mary).** THE WORKS. Edited with an Introduction and Notes by E. V. LUCAS. *A New and Revised Edition in Six Volumes.* With Frontispiece. *Fcap 8vo.* 5s. *each*. The volumes are:—
I. MISCELLANEOUS PROSE. II. ELIA AND THE LAST ESSAYS OF ELIA. III. BOOKS FOR CHILDREN. IV. PLAYS AND POEMS. V. and VI. LETTERS.

Lane-Poole (Stanley). A HISTORY OF EGYPT IN THE MIDDLE AGES. Illustrated. *Cr. 8vo.* 6s.

Lankester (Sir Ray). SCIENCE FROM AN EASY CHAIR. Illustrated. *Fifth Edition. Cr. 8vo.* 6s.

Le Braz (Anatole). THE LAND OF PARDONS. Translated by FRANCES M. GOSTLING. Illustrated. *Third Edition. Cr. 8vo.* 6s.

Lindsay (Mabel M.). ANNI DOMINI: A Gospel Study. With Maps. *Two Volumes. Super Royal 8vo.* 10s. *net.*

Lock (Walter). ST. PAUL, THE MASTER-BUILDER. *Third Edition. Cr. 8vo.* 3s. 6d.
THE BIBLE AND CHRISTIAN LIFE. *Cr. 8vo.* 6s.

Lodge (Sir Oliver). THE SUBSTANCE OF FAITH, ALLIED WITH SCIENCE: A Catechism for Parents and Teachers. *Eleventh Edition. Cr. 8vo.* 2s. *net.*
MAN AND THE UNIVERSE: A Study of the Influence of the Advance in Scientific Knowledge upon our understanding of Christianity. *Ninth Edition. Demy 8vo.* 5s. *net.*
THE SURVIVAL OF MAN. A Study in Unrecognised Human Faculty. *Fifth Edition. Wide Crown 8vo.* 5s. *net.*
REASON AND BELIEF. *Fifth Edition. Cr. 8vo.* 3s. 6d. *net.*

Lorimer (George Horace). LETTERS FROM A SELF-MADE MERCHANT TO HIS SON. Illustrated. *Twenty-second Edition. Cr. 8vo.* 3s. 6d.
OLD GORGON GRAHAM. Illustrated. *Second Edition. Cr. 8vo.* 6s.

'Loyal Serviteur.' THE STORY OF BAYARD. Adapted by Amy G. Andrewes. Illustrated. *Cr. 8vo.* 2s. 6d.

Lucas (E. V.). THE LIFE OF CHARLES LAMB. Illustrated. *Fifth Edition. Demy 8vo.* 7s. 6d. *net.*
A WANDERER IN HOLLAND. Illustrated. *Thirteenth Edition. Cr. 8vo.* 6s.
Also Fcap. 8vo. 5s.
A WANDERER IN LONDON. Illustrated. *Twelfth Edition. Cr. 8vo.* 6s.
Also Fcap. 8vo. 5s.
A WANDERER IN PARIS. Illustrated. *Ninth Edition. Cr. 8vo.* 6s.
Also Seventh Edition. Fcap. 8vo. 5s.
THE OPEN ROAD: A Little Book for Wayfarers. *Eighteenth Edition. Fcap. 8vo.* 5s.; India Paper, 7s. 6d.
THE FRIENDLY TOWN: a Little Book for the Urbane. *Sixth Edition. Fcap. 8vo.* 5s.; India Paper, 7s. 6d.
FIRESIDE AND SUNSHINE. *Sixth Edition. Fcap. 8vo.* 5s.
CHARACTER AND COMEDY. *Sixth Edition. Fcap. 8vo.* 5s.
THE GENTLEST ART. A Choice of Letters by Entertaining Hands. *Seventh Edition. Fcap. 8vo.* 5s.
THE SECOND POST. *Third Edition. Fcap. 8vo.* 5s.
A SWAN AND HER FRIENDS. Illustrated. *Demy 8vo.* 12s. 6d. *net.*
HER INFINITE VARIETY: A Feminine Portrait Gallery. *Sixth Edition. Fcap. 8vo.* 5s.

GOOD COMPANY: A Rally of Men. *Second Edition. Fcap. 8vo.* 5s.
ONE DAY AND ANOTHER. *Fifth Edition. Fcap. 8vo.* 5s.
OLD LAMPS FOR NEW. *Fourth Edition. Fcap. 8vo.* 5s.
LISTENER'S LURE: An Oblique Narration. *Ninth Edition. Fcap. 8vo.* 5s.
OVER BEMERTON'S: An Easy-Going Chronicle. *Ninth Edition. Fcap. 8vo.* 5s.
MR. INGLESIDE. *Ninth Edition. Fcap. 8vo.* 5s.
See also Lamb (Charles).

*Lydekker (R. and Others). REPTILES, AMPHIBIA, AND FISHES. Illustrated. *Demy 8vo.* 10s. 6d. *net.*

Lydekker (R.). THE OX. Illustrated. *Cr. 8vo.* 6s.

Macaulay (Lord). CRITICAL AND HISTORICAL ESSAYS. Edited by F. C. Montague. *Three Volumes. Cr. 8vo.* 18s.

McCabe (Joseph). THE DECAY OF THE CHURCH OF ROME. *Third Edition. Demy 8vo.* 7s. 6d. *net.*
THE EMPRESSES OF ROME. Illustrated. *Demy 8vo.* 12s. 6d. *net.*

MacCarthy (Desmond) and Russell (Agatha). LADY JOHN RUSSELL: A Memoir. Illustrated. *Fourth Edition. Demy 8vo.* 10s. 6d. *net.*

McCullagh (Francis). THE FALL OF ABD-UL-HAMID. Illustrated. *Demy 8vo.* 10s. 6d. *net.*

*MacDonagh (Michael). THE SPEAKER OF THE HOUSE. *Demy 8vo.* 10s. 6d. *net.*

McDougall (William). AN INTRODUCTION TO SOCIAL PSYCHOLOGY. *Fourth Edition. Cr. 8vo.* 5s. *net.*
BODY AND MIND: A History and a Defence of Animism. *Demy 8vo.* 10s. 6d. *net.*

*'Mdlle. Mori'(Author of). ST. CATHERINE OF SIENA AND HER TIMES. Illustrated. *Second Edition. Demy 8vo.* 7s. 6d. *net.*

Maeterlinck (Maurice). THE BLUE BIRD: A Fairy Play in Six Acts. Translated by Alexander Teixeira de Mattos. *Twentieth Edition. Fcap. 8vo. Deckle Edges.* 3s. 6d. *net. Also Twenty-seventh Edition. Fcap. 8vo. Cloth,* 1s. *net.*
THE BLUE BIRD: A Fairy Play in Six Acts. Translated by Alexander Teixeira de Mattos. Illustrated. *Twenty-fifth Edition. Cr. 4to.* 21s. *net.*
MARY MAGDALENE: A Play in Three Acts. Translated by Alexander Teixeira de Mattos. *Third Edition. Fcap. 8vo. Deckle Edges.* 3s. 6d. *net.*

General Literature

Mahaffy (J. P.). A HISTORY OF EGYPT UNDER THE PTOLEMAIC DYNASTY. Illustrated. *Cr. 8vo. 6s.*

Maitland (F. W.). ROMAN CANON LAW IN THE CHURCH OF ENGLAND. *Royal 8vo. 7s. 6d.*

Marett (R. R.). THE THRESHOLD OF RELIGION. *Cr. 8vo. 3s. 6d. net.*

Marriott (Charles). A SPANISH HOLIDAY. Illustrated. *Demy 8vo. 7s. 6d. net.*
THE ROMANCE OF THE RHINE. Illustrated. *Demy 8vo. 10s. 6d. net.*

Marriott (J. A. R.). THE LIFE AND TIMES OF LUCIUS CARY, VISCOUNT FALKLAND. Illustrated. *Second Edition. Demy 8vo. 7s. 6d. net.*

Masefield (John). SEA LIFE IN NELSON'S TIME. Illustrated. *Cr. 8vo. 3s. 6d. net.*
A SAILOR'S GARLAND. Selected and Edited. *Second Edition. Cr. 8vo. 3s. 6d. net.*

Masterman (C. F. G.). TENNYSON AS A RELIGIOUS TEACHER. *Second Edition. Cr. 8vo. 6s.*
THE CONDITION OF ENGLAND. *Fourth Edition. Cr. 8vo. 6s.*

Medley (D. J.). ORIGINAL ILLUSTRATIONS OF ENGLISH CONSTITUTIONAL HISTORY. *Cr. 8vo. 7s. 6d. net.*

Meldrum (D. S.). HOME LIFE IN HOLLAND. Illustrated. *Second Edition. Demy 8vo. 10s. 6d. net.*

Methuen (A. M. S.). ENGLAND'S RUIN: Discussed in Fourteen Letters to a Protectionist. *Ninth Edition. Cr. 8vo. 3d. net.*

Meynell (Everard). COROT AND HIS FRIENDS. Illustrated. *Demy 8vo. 10s. 6d. net.*

Miles (Eustace). LIFE AFTER LIFE: or, The Theory of Reincarnation. *Cr. 8vo. 2s. 6d. net.*
THE POWER OF CONCENTRATION: How to Acquire it. *Third Edition. Cr. 8vo. 3s. 6d. net.*

Millais (J. G.). THE LIFE AND LETTERS OF SIR JOHN EVERETT MILLAIS. Illustrated. *New Edition. Demy 8vo. 7s. 6d. net.*

Milne (J. G.). A HISTORY OF EGYPT UNDER ROMAN RULE. Illustrated. *Cr. 8vo. 6s.*

Moffat (Mary M.). QUEEN LOUISA OF PRUSSIA. Illustrated. *Fourth Edition. Cr. 8vo. 6s.*
MARIA THERESA. Illustrated. *10s. 6d. net.*

Money (L. G. Chiozza). RICHES AND POVERTY, 1910. *Tenth and Revised Edition. Demy 8vo. 5s. net.*
MONEY'S FISCAL DICTIONARY, 1910. *Second Edition. Demy 8vo. 5s. net.*

Montague (C. E.). DRAMATIC VALUES. *Second Edition. Fcap. 8vo. 5s.*

Moorhouse (E. Hallam). NELSON'S LADY HAMILTON. Illustrated. *Third Edition. Demy 8vo. 7s. 6d. net.*

Morgan (J. H.). THE HOUSE OF LORDS AND THE CONSTITUTION. With an Introduction by the Lord Chancellor. *Cr. 8vo. 1s. net.*

Nevill (Lady Dorothy). UNDER FIVE REIGNS. Edited by her son. Illustrated. *Fifth Edition. Demy 8vo. 15s. net.*

Norway (A. H.). NAPLES. Past and Present. Illustrated. *Fourth Edition. Cr. 8vo. 6s.*

Oman (C. W. C.). A HISTORY OF THE ART OF WAR IN THE MIDDLE AGES. Illustrated. *Demy 8vo. 10s. 6d. net.*
ENGLAND BEFORE THE NORMAN CONQUEST. With Maps. *Second Edition. Demy 8vo. 10s. 6d. net.*

Oxford (M. N.). A HANDBOOK OF NURSING. *Fifth Edition. Cr. 8vo. 3s. 6d.*

Pakes (W. C. C.). THE SCIENCE OF HYGIENE. Illustrated. *Second and Cheaper Edition. Cr. 8vo. 5s. net.*

Parker (Eric). THE BOOK OF THE ZOO; By Day and Night. Illustrated. *Second Edition. Cr. 8vo. 6s.*

Pears (Sir Edwin). TURKEY AND ITS PEOPLE. *Second Edition. Demy 8vo. 12s. 6d. net.*

Petrie (W. M. Flinders). A HISTORY OF EGYPT. Illustrated. *In Six Volumes. Cr. 8vo. 6s. each.*
Vol. I. From the Ist to the XVIth Dynasty. *Seventh Edition.*
Vol. II. The XVIIth and XVIIIth Dynasties. *Fourth Edition.*
Vol. III. XIXth to XXXth Dynasties.
Vol. IV. Egypt under the Ptolemaic Dynasty. J. P. Mahaffy.
Vol. V. Egypt under Roman Rule. J. G. Milne.
Vol. VI. Egypt in the Middle Ages. Stanley Lane-Poole.
RELIGION AND CONSCIENCE IN ANCIENT EGYPT. Illustrated *Cr. 8vo. 2s. 6d.*
SYRIA AND EGYPT, FROM THE TELL EL AMARNA LETTERS. *Cr. 8vo. 2s. 6d.*

EGYPTIAN TALES. Translated from the Papyri. First Series, ivth to xiith Dynasty. Illustrated. *Second Edition.* *Cr. 8vo.* 3s. 6d.

EGYPTIAN TALES. Translated from the Papyri. Second Series, xviiith to xixth Dynasty. Illustrated. *Cr. 8vo.* 3s. 6d.

EGYPTIAN DECORATIVE ART. Illustrated. *Cr. 8vo.* 3s. 6d.

Phelps (Ruth S.). SKIES ITALIAN: A LITTLE BREVIARY FOR TRAVELLERS IN ITALY. *Fcap. 8vo.* 5s. net.

Podmore (Frank). MODERN SPIRITUALISM. *Two Volumes.* *Demy 8vo.* 21s. net.

MESMERISM AND CHRISTIAN SCIENCE: A Short History of Mental Healing. *Second Edition.* *Demy 8vo.* 10s. 6d. net.

Pollard (Alfred W.). SHAKESPEARE FOLIOS AND QUARTOS. A Study in the Bibliography of Shakespeare's Plays, 1594-1685. Illustrated. *Folio.* 21s. net.

*Porter (G. R.). THE PROGRESS OF THE NATION. A New Edition. Edited by F. W. HIRST. *Demy 8vo.* 21s. net.

Powell (Arthur E.). FOOD AND HEALTH. *Cr. 8vo.* 3s. 6d. net.

Power (J. O'Connor). THE MAKING OF AN ORATOR. *Cr. 8vo.* 6s.

*Price (Eleanor C.). CARDINAL DE RICHELIEU. Illustrated. *Second Edition.* *Demy 8vo.* 10s. 6d. net.

Price (L. L.), A SHORT HISTORY OF POLITICAL ECONOMY IN ENGLAND FROM ADAM SMITH TO ARNOLD TOYNBEE. *Seventh Edition.* *Cr. 8vo.* 2s. 6d.

Pycraft (W. P.). A HISTORY OF BIRDS. Illustrated. *Demy 8vo.* 10s. 6d. net.

*Rappoport (Angelo S.). HOME LIFE IN RUSSIA. Illustrated. *Demy 8vo.* 10s. 6d. net.

Rawlings (Gertrude B.). COINS AND HOW TO KNOW THEM. Illustrated. *Third Edition.* *Cr. 8vo.* 6s.

Read (C. Stanford), FADS AND FEEDING. *Cr. 8vo.* 2s. 6d. net.

Regan (C. Tate). THE FRESHWATER FISHES OF THE BRITISH ISLES. Illustrated. *Cr. 8vo.* 6s.

Reid (Archdall), THE LAWS OF HEREDITY. *Second Edition.* *Demy 8vo.* 21s. net.

Robertson (C. Grant). SELECT STATUTES, CASES, AND DOCUMENTS, 1660-1894. *Demy 8vo.* 10s. 6d. net.

ENGLAND UNDER THE HANOVERIANS. Illustrated. *Second Edition.* *Demy 8vo.* 10s. 6d. net.

Roe (Fred). OLD OAK FURNITURE. Illustrated. *Second Edition.* *Demy 8vo.* 10s. 6d. net.

Royde-Smith (N. G.). THE PILLOW BOOK: A GARNER OF MANY MOODS. Collected. *Second Edition.* *Cr. 8vo.* 4s. 6d. net.

POETS OF OUR DAY. Selected, with an Introduction. *Fcap. 8vo.* 5s.

Russell (W. Clark). THE LIFE OF ADMIRAL LORD COLLINGWOOD. Illustrated. *Fourth Edition.* *Cr. 8vo.* 6s.

*Ryan (P. F. W.). STUART LIFE AND MANNERS; A Social History. Illustrated. *Demy 8vo.* 10s. 6d. net.

St. Francis of Assisi. THE LITTLE FLOWERS OF THE GLORIOUS MESSER, AND OF HIS FRIARS. Done into English, with Notes by WILLIAM HEYWOOD. Illustrated. *Demy 8vo.* 5s. net.

'Saki' (H. H. Munro). REGINALD. *Third Edition.* *Fcap. 8vo.* 2s. 6d. net.

REGINALD IN RUSSIA. *Fcap. 8vo.* 2s. 6d. net.

Sandeman (G. A. C.). METTERNICH. Illustrated. *Demy 8vo.* 10s. 6d. net.

Selous (Edmund). TOMMY SMITH'S ANIMALS. Illustrated. *Eleventh Edition.* *Fcap. 8vo.* 2s. 6d.

TOMMY SMITH'S OTHER ANIMALS. Illustrated. *Fifth Edition.* *Fcap. 8vo.* 2s. 6d.

JACK'S INSECTS. Illustrated. *Cr. 8vo.* 6s.

Shakespeare (William).
THE FOUR FOLIOS, 1623; 1632; 1664; 1685. Each £4 4s. net, or a complete set, £12 12s. net.

THE POEMS OF WILLIAM SHAKESPEARE. With an Introduction and Notes by GEORGE WYNDHAM. *Demy 8vo.* Buckram. 10s. 6d.

Sharp (A.). VICTORIAN POETS. *Cr. 8vo.* 2s. 6d.

Sidgwick (Mrs. Alfred). HOME LIFE IN GERMANY. Illustrated. *Second Edition.* *Demy 8vo.* 10s. 6d. net.

Sladen (Douglas). SICILY: The New Winter Resort. Illustrated. *Second Edition.* *Cr. 8vo.* 5s. net.

Smith (Adam). THE WEALTH OF NATIONS. Edited by EDWIN CANNAN. *Two Volumes.* *Demy 8vo.* 21s. net.

*Smith (G. Herbert). GEMS AND PRECIOUS STONES. Illustrated. *Cr. 8vo.* 6s.

Snell (F. J.). A BOOK OF EXMOOR. Illustrated. *Cr. 8vo.* 6s.

General Literature

'Stancliffe.' GOLF DO'S AND DONT'S. *Fourth Edition. Fcap. 8vo.* 1s. *net.*

Stevenson (R. L.). THE LETTERS OF ROBERT LOUIS STEVENSON. Edited by Sir SIDNEY COLVIN. A New and Enlarged Edition in 4 volumes. *Third Edition. Fcap. 8vo. Leather, each* 5s. *net.*
VAILIMA LETTERS. With an Etched Portrait by WILLIAM STRANG. *Ninth Edition. Cr. 8vo. Buckram,* 6s.
THE LIFE OF R. L. STEVENSON. See BALFOUR (G.).

Stevenson (M. I.). FROM SARANAC TO THE MARQUESAS AND BEYOND. Being Letters written by Mrs. M. I. STEVENSON during 1887-88. *Cr. 8vo.* 6s. *net.*
LETTERS FROM SAMOA, 1891-95. Edited and arranged by M. C. BALFOUR. Illustrated. *Second Edition. Cr. 8vo.* 6s. *net.*

Storr (Vernon F.). DEVELOPMENT AND DIVINE PURPOSE. *Cr. 8vo.* 5s. *net.*

Streatfeild (R. A.). MODERN MUSIC AND MUSICIANS. Illustrated. *Second Edition. Demy 8vo.* 7s. 6d. *net.*

Swanton (E. W.). FUNGI AND HOW TO KNOW THEM. Illustrated. *Cr. 8vo.* 6s. *net.*

Sykes (Ella C.). PERSIA AND ITS PEOPLE. Illustrated. *Demy 8vo.* 10s. 6d. *net.*

Symes (J. E.). THE FRENCH REVOLUTION. *Second Edition. Cr. 8vo.* 2s. 6d.

Tabor (Margaret E.). THE SAINTS IN ART. Illustrated. *Fcap. 8vo.* 3s. 6d. *net.*

Taylor (A. E.). THE ELEMENTS OF METAPHYSICS. *Second Edition. Demy 8vo.* 10s. 6d. *net.*

Thibaudeau (A. C.). BONAPARTE AND THE CONSULATE. Translated and Edited by G. K. FORTESCUE. Illustrated. *Demy 8vo.* 10s. 6d. *net.*

Thomas (Edward). MAURICE MAETERLINCK. Illustrated. *Second Edition. Cr. 8vo.* 5s. *net.*

Thompson (Francis). SELECTED POEMS OF FRANCIS THOMPSON. With a Biographical Note by WILFRID MEYNELL. With a Portrait in Photogravure. *Seventh Edition. Fcap. 8vo.* 5s. *net.*

Tileston (Mary W.). DAILY STRENGTH FOR DAILY NEEDS. *Eighteenth Edition. Medium 16mo.* 2s. 6d. *net.* Lambskin 3s. 6d. *net.* Also an edition in superior binding, 6s.
THE STRONGHOLD OF HOPE. *Medium 16mo.* 2s. 6d. *net.*

Toynbee (Paget). DANTE ALIGHIERI; HIS LIFE AND WORKS. With 16 Illustrations. *Fourth and Enlarged Edition. Cr. 8vo.* 5s. *net.*

Trench (Herbert.) DEIRDRE WEDDED, AND OTHER POEMS. *Second and Revised Edition. Large Post 8vo.* 6s.
NEW POEMS. *Second Edition. Large Post 8vo.* 6s.
APOLLO AND THE SEAMAN. *Large Post 8vo. Paper,* 1s. 6d. *net;* cloth, 2s. 6d. *net.*

Trevelyan (G. M.). ENGLAND UNDER THE STUARTS. With Maps and Plans. *Fifth Edition. Demy 8vo.* 10s. 6d. *net.*

Triggs (Inigo H.). TOWN PLANNING: PAST, PRESENT, AND POSSIBLE. Illustrated. *Second Edition. Wide Royal 8vo.* 15s. *net.*

Underhill (Evelyn). MYSTICISM. A Study in the Nature and Development of Man's Spiritual Consciousness. *Third Edition. Demy 8vo.* 15s. *net.*

Vaughan (Herbert M.). THE NAPLES RIVIERA. Illustrated. *Second Edition. Cr. 8vo.* 6s.
FLORENCE AND HER TREASURES. Illustrated. *Fcap. 8vo.* 5s. *net.*

Vernon (Hon. W. Warren). READINGS ON THE INFERNO OF DANTE. With an Introduction by the REV. DR. MOORE. *Two Volumes. Second Edition. Cr. 8vo.* 15s. *net.*
READINGS ON THE PURGATORIO OF DANTE. With an Introduction by the late DEAN CHURCH. *Two Volumes. Third Edition. Cr. 8vo.* 15s. *net.*
READINGS ON THE PARADISO OF DANTE. With an Introduction by the BISHOP OF RIPON. *Two Volumes. Second Edition. Cr. 8vo.* 15s. *net.*

Waddell (Col. L. A.). LHASA AND ITS MYSTERIES. With a Record of the Expedition of 1903-1904. Illustrated. *Third and Cheaper Edition. Medium 8vo.* 7s. 6d. *net.*

Wagner (Richard). RICHARD WAGNER'S MUSIC DRAMAS: Interpretations, embodying Wagner's own explanations. By ALICE LEIGHTON CLEATHER and BASIL CRUMP. *Fcap. 8vo.* 2s. 6d. *each.*
THE RING OF THE NIBELUNG. *Fifth Edition.*
TRISTAN AND ISOLDE.

Waterhouse (Elizabeth). WITH THE SIMPLE-HEARTED: Little Homilies to Women in Country Places. *Third Edition. Small Pott 8vo.* 2s. *net.*
THE HOUSE BY THE CHERRY TREE. A Second Series of Little Homilies to Women in Country Places. *Small Pott 8vo.* 2s. *net.*
COMPANIONS OF THE WAY. Being Selections for Morning and Evening Reading. Chosen and arranged by ELIZABETH WATERHOUSE. *Large Cr. 8vo.* 5s. *net.*
THOUGHTS OF A TERTIARY. *Small Pott 8vo.* 1s. *net.*

Waters (W. G.). ITALIAN SCULPTORS AND SMITHS. Illustrated. *Cr. 8vo.* 7s. 6d. net.

*Watt (Francis). EDINBURGH AND THE LOTHIANS. Illustrated. *Second Edition. Cr. 8vo.* 7s. 6d. net.

Weigall (Arthur E. P.). A GUIDE TO THE ANTIQUITIES OF UPPER EGYPT: From Abydos to the Sudan Frontier. Illustrated. *Cr. 8vo.* 7s. 6d. net.

Welch (Catharine). THE LITTLE DAUPHIN. Illustrated. *Cr. 8vo.* 6s.

Wells (J.). OXFORD AND OXFORD LIFE. *Third Edition. Cr. 8vo.* 3s. 6d.
A SHORT HISTORY OF ROME. *Eleventh Edition.* With 3 Maps. *Cr. 8vo.* 3s. 6d.

Westell (W. Percival). THE YOUNG NATURALIST. Illustrated. *Cr. 8vo.* 6s.
THE YOUNG ORNITHOLOGIST. Illustrated. *Cr. 8vo.* 5s.

Westell (W. Percival), and Cooper (C. S.). THE YOUNG BOTANIST. Illustrated. *Cr. 8vo.* 3s. 6d. net.

White (George F.). A CENTURY OF SPAIN AND PORTUGAL, 1788-1898. *Demy 8vo.* 12s. 6d. net.

Wilde (Oscar). DE PROFUNDIS. *Twelfth Edition. Cr. 8vo.* 5s. net.
THE WORKS OF OSCAR WILDE. *In Twelve Volumes. Fcap. 8vo.* 5s. net each volume.
  I. LORD ARTHUR SAVILE'S CRIME AND THE PORTRAIT OF MR. W. H. II. THE DUCHESS OF PADUA. III. POEMS. IV. LADY WINDERMERE'S FAN. V. A WOMAN OF NO IMPORTANCE. VI. AN IDEAL HUSBAND. VII. THE IMPORTANCE OF BEING EARNEST. VIII. A HOUSE OF POMEGRANATES. IX. INTENTIONS. X. DE PROFUNDIS AND PRISON LETTERS. XI. ESSAYS. XII. SALOMÉ, A FLORENTINE TRAGEDY, and LA SAINTE COURTISANE.

Williams (H. Noel). THE WOMEN BONAPARTES. The Mother and three Sisters of Napoleon. Illustrated. *In Two Volumes. Demy 8vo.* 24s. net.
A ROSE OF SAVOY: MARIE ADÉLAÏDE OF SAVOY, DUCHESSE DE BOURGOGNE, MOTHER OF LOUIS XV. Illustrated. *Second Edition. Demy 8vo.* 15s. net.
THE FASCINATING DUC DE RICHELIEU: LOUIS FRANÇOIS ARMAND DU PLESSIS (1696-1788). Illustrated. *Demy 8vo.* 15s. net.
A PRINCESS OF ADVENTURE: MARIE CAROLINE, DUCHESSE DE BERRY (1798-1870). Illustrated. *Demy 8vo.* 15s. net.

Wood (Sir Evelyn). FROM MIDSHIPMAN TO FIELD-MARSHAL. Illustrated. *Fifth and Cheaper Edition. Demy 8vo.* 7s. 6d. net.
THE REVOLT IN HINDUSTAN. 1857-59. Illustrated. *Second Edition. Cr. 8vo.* 6s.

Wood (W. Birkbeck), and Edmonds (Lieut.-Col. J. E.). A HISTORY OF THE CIVIL WAR IN THE UNITED STATES (1861-5). With an Introduction by H. SPENSER WILKINSON. With 24 Maps and Plans. *Third Edition. Demy 8vo.* 12s. 6d. net.

Wordsworth (W.). THE POEMS. With an Introduction and Notes by NOWELL C. SMITH. *In Three Volumes. Demy 8vo.* 15s. net.

Wyllie (M. A.). NORWAY AND ITS FJORDS. Illustrated. *Second Edition. Cr. 8vo.* 6s.

Yeats (W. B.). A BOOK OF IRISH VERSE. *Third Edition. Cr. 8vo.* 3s. 6d.

PART II.—A SELECTION OF SERIES.

Ancient Cities.

General Editor, B. C. A. WINDLE.

Cr. 8vo. 4s. 6d. net each volume.

With Illustrations by E. H. NEW, and other Artists.

BRISTOL. Alfred Harvey.
CANTERBURY. J. C. Cox.
CHESTER. B. C. A. Windle.
DUBLIN. S. A. O. Fitzpatrick.

EDINBURGH. M. G. Williamson.
LINCOLN. E. Mansel Sympson.
SHREWSBURY. T. Auden.
WELLS and GLASTONBURY. T. S. Holmes.

The Antiquary's Books.

General Editor, J. CHARLES COX.

Demy 8vo.   7s. 6d. net each volume.

With Numerous Illustrations.

ARCHÆOLOGY AND FALSE ANTIQUITIES. R. Munro.
BELLS OF ENGLAND, THE. Canon J. J. Raven. *Second Edition.*
BRASSES OF ENGLAND, THE. Herbert W. Macklin. *Second Edition.*
CELTIC ART IN PAGAN AND CHRISTIAN TIMES. J. Romilly Allen. *Second Edition.*
CASTLES AND WALLED TOWNS OF ENGLAND. A. Harvey.
DOMESDAY INQUEST, THE. Adolphus Ballard.
ENGLISH CHURCH FURNITURE. J. C. Cox and A. Harvey. *Second Edition.*
ENGLISH COSTUME. From Prehistoric Times to the End of the Eighteenth Century. George Clinch.
ENGLISH MONASTIC LIFE. The Right Rev. Abbot Gasquet. *Fourth Edition.*
ENGLISH SEALS. J. Harvey Bloom.
FOLK-LORE AS AN HISTORICAL SCIENCE. Sir G. L. Gomme.
GILDS AND COMPANIES OF LONDON, THE. George Unwin.
MANOR AND MANORIAL RECORDS, THE. Nathaniel J. Hone.
MEDIÆVAL HOSPITALS OF ENGLAND, THE. Rotha Mary Clay.
OLD ENGLISH INSTRUMENTS OF MUSIC. F. W. Galpin. *Second Edition.*
OLD ENGLISH LIBRARIES. James Hutt.
OLD SERVICE BOOKS OF THE ENGLISH CHURCH. Christopher Wordsworth, and Henry Littlehales. *Second Edition.*
PARISH LIFE IN MEDIÆVAL ENGLAND. The Right Rev. Abbot Gasquet. *Third Edition.*
PARISH REGISTERS OF ENGLAND, THE. J. C. Cox.
REMAINS OF THE PREHISTORIC AGE IN ENGLAND. B. C. A. Windle. *Second Edition.*
ROMAN ERA IN BRITAIN, THE. J. Ward.
ROMAN-BRITISH BUILDINGS AND EARTH-WORKS. J. Ward.
ROYAL FORESTS OF ENGLAND, THE. J. C. Cox.
SHRINES OF BRITISH SAINTS. J. C. Wall.

The Arden Shakespeare.

Demy 8vo.   2s. 6d. net each volume.

An edition of Shakespeare in single Plays; each edited with a full Introduction, Textual Notes, and a Commentary at the foot of the page.

ALL'S WELL THAT ENDS WELL.
ANTONY AND CLEOPATRA.
CYMBELINE.
COMEDY OF ERRORS, THE.
HAMLET. *Third Edition.*
JULIUS CAESAR.
KING HENRY IV. PT. I.
KING HENRY V.
KING HENRY VI. PT. I.
KING HENRY VI. PT. II.
KING HENRY VI. PT. III.
KING LEAR.
KING RICHARD III.
LIFE AND DEATH OF KING JOHN, THE.
LOVE'S LABOUR'S LOST.
MACBETH.
MEASURE FOR MEASURE.
MERCHANT OF VENICE, THE.
MERRY WIVES OF WINDSOR, THE.
MIDSUMMER NIGHT'S DREAM, A.
OTHELLO.
PERICLES.
ROMEO AND JULIET.
TAMING OF THE SHREW, THE.
TEMPEST, THE.
TIMON OF ATHENS.
TITUS ANDRONICUS.
TROILUS AND CRESSIDA.
TWO GENTLEMEN OF VERONA, THE.
TWELFTH NIGHT.
VENUS AND ADONIS.

Classics of Art.

Edited by Dr. J. H. W. LAING.

With numerous Illustrations. Wide Royal 8vo.

THE ART OF THE GREEKS. H. B. Walters. 12s. 6d. net.
THE ART OF THE ROMANS. H. B. Walters. 15s. net.
CHARDIN. H. E. A. Furst. 12s. 6d. net.
DONATELLO. Maud Cruttwell. 15s. net.
FLORENTINE SCULPTORS OF THE RENAISSANCE. Wilhelm Bode. Translated by Jessie Haynes. 12s. 6d. net.
GEORGE ROMNEY. Arthur B. Chamberlain. 12s. 6d. net.
GHIRLANDAIO. Gerald S. Davies. *Second Edition.* 10s. 6d.

MICHELANGELO. Gerald S. Davies. 12s. 6d. net.
RUBENS. Edward Dillon, 25s. net.
RAPHAEL. A. P. Oppé. 12s. 6d. net.
REMBRANDT'S ETCHINGS. A. M. Hind.
TITIAN. Charles Ricketts. 12s. 6d. net.
TINTORETTO. Evelyn March Phillipps. 15s. net.
TURNER'S SKETCHES AND DRAWINGS. A. J. Finberg. 12s. 6d. net. *Second Edition.*
VELAZQUEZ. A. de Beruete. 10s. 6d. net.

The Complete Series.

Fully Illustrated. Demy 8vo.

THE COMPLETE BILLIARD PLAYER. Charles Roberts. 10s. 6d. net.
THE COMPLETE COOK. Lilian Whitling. 7s. 6d. net.
THE COMPLETE CRICKETER. Albert E. Knight. 7s. 6d. net. *Second Edition.*
THE COMPLETE FOXHUNTER. Charles Richardson. 12s. 6d. net. *Second Edition.*
THE COMPLETE GOLFER. Harry Vardon. 10s. 6d. net. *Twelfth Edition.*
THE COMPLETE HOCKEY-PLAYER. Eustace E. White. 5s. net. *Second Edition.*
THE COMPLETE LAWN TENNIS PLAYER. A. Wallis Myers. 10s. 6d. net. *Third Edition, Revised.*

THE COMPLETE MOTORIST. Filson Young. 12s. 6d. net. *New Edition (Seventh).*
THE COMPLETE MOUNTAINEER. G. D. Abraham. 15s. net. *Second Edition.*
THE COMPLETE OARSMAN. R. C. Lehmann. 10s. 6d. net.
THE COMPLETE PHOTOGRAPHER. R. Child Bayley. 10s. 6d. net. *Fourth Edition.*
THE COMPLETE RUGBY FOOTBALLER, ON THE NEW ZEALAND SYSTEM. D. Gallaher and W. J. Stead. 10s. 6d. net. *Second Edition.*
THE COMPLETE SHOT. G. T. Teasdale Buckell. 12s. 6d. net. *Third Edition.*

The Connoisseur's Library.

With numerous Illustrations. Wide Royal 8vo. 25s. net each volume.

ENGLISH FURNITURE. F. S. Robinson.
ENGLISH COLOURED BOOKS. Martin Hardie.
ETCHINGS. Sir F. Wedmore.
EUROPEAN ENAMELS. Henry H. Cunynghame.
GLASS. Edward Dillon.
GOLDSMITHS' AND SILVERSMITHS' WORK. Nelson Dawson. *Second Edition.*
ILLUMINATED MANUSCRIPTS. J. A. Herbert. *Second Edition.*

IVORIES. Alfred Maskell.
JEWELLERY. H. Clifford Smith. *Second Edition.*
MEZZOTINTS. Cyril Davenport.
MINIATURES. Dudley Heath.
PORCELAIN. Edward Dillon.
SEALS. Walter de Gray Birch.
WOOD SCULPTURE. Alfred Maskell. *Second Edition.*

Handbooks of English Church History.

Edited by J. H. BURN. *Crown 8vo.* 2s. 6d. *net each volume.*

THE FOUNDATIONS OF THE ENGLISH CHURCH. J. H. Maude.
THE SAXON CHURCH AND THE NORMAN CONQUEST. C. T. Cruttwell.
THE MEDIÆVAL CHURCH AND THE PAPACY. A. C. Jennings.

THE REFORMATION PERIOD. Henry Gee.
THE STRUGGLE WITH PURITANISM. Bruce Blaxland.
THE CHURCH OF ENGLAND IN THE EIGHTEENTH CENTURY. Alfred Plummer.

Handbooks of Theology.

THE DOCTRINE OF THE INCARNATION. R. L. Ottley. *Fifth Edition, Revised. Demy 8vo.* 12s. 6d.
A HISTORY OF EARLY CHRISTIAN DOCTRINE. J. F. Bethune-Baker. *Demy 8vo.* 10s. 6d.
AN INTRODUCTION TO THE HISTORY OF RELIGION. F. B. Jevons. *Fifth Edition. Demy 8vo.* 10s. 6d.

AN INTRODUCTION TO THE HISTORY OF THE CREEDS. A. E. Burn. *Demy 8vo.* 10s. 6d.
THE PHILOSOPHY OF RELIGION IN ENGLAND AND AMERICA. Alfred Caldecott. *Demy 8vo.* 10s. 6d.
THE XXXIX. ARTICLES OF THE CHURCH OF ENGLAND. Edited by E. C. S. Gibson, *Seventh Edition. Demy 8vo.* 12s. 6d.

The Illustrated Pocket Library of Plain and Coloured Books.

Fcap. 8vo. 3s. 6d. *net each volume.*

WITH COLOURED ILLUSTRATIONS.

OLD COLOURED BOOKS. George Paston. 2s. net.
THE LIFE AND DEATH OF JOHN MYTTON, ESQ. Nimrod. *Fifth Edition.*
THE LIFE OF A SPORTSMAN. Nimrod.
HANDLEY CROSS. R. S. Surtees. *Fourth Edition.*
MR. SPONGE'S SPORTING TOUR. R. S. Surtees. *Second Edition.*
JORROCKS'S JAUNTS AND JOLLITIES. R. S. Surtees. *Third Edition.*
ASK MAMMA. R. S. Surtees.
THE ANALYSIS OF THE HUNTING FIELD. R. S. Surtees.
THE TOUR OF DR. SYNTAX IN SEARCH OF THE PICTURESQUE. William Combe.
THE TOUR OF DR. SYNTAX IN SEARCH OF CONSOLATION. William Combe.
THE THIRD TOUR OF DR. SYNTAX IN SEARCH OF A WIFE. William Combe.
THE HISTORY OF JOHNNY QUAE GENUS. the Author of 'The Three Tours.'
THE ENGLISH DANCE OF DEATH, from the Designs of T. Rowlandson, with Metrical Illustrations by the Author of 'Doctor Syntax.' *Two Volumes.*

THE DANCE OF LIFE: A Poem. The Author of 'Dr. Syntax.'
LIFE IN LONDON. Pierce Egan.
REAL LIFE IN LONDON. An Amateur (Pierce Egan). *Two Volumes.*
THE LIFE OF AN ACTOR. Pierce Egan.
THE VICAR OF WAKEFIELD. Oliver Goldsmith.
THE MILITARY ADVENTURES OF JOHNNY NEWCOMBE. An Officer.
THE NATIONAL SPORTS OF GREAT BRITAIN. With Descriptions and 50 Coloured Plates by Henry Alken.
THE ADVENTURES OF A POST CAPTAIN. A Naval Officer.
GAMONIA. Lawrence Rawstorne.
AN ACADEMY FOR GROWN HORSEMEN. Geoffrey Gambado.
REAL LIFE IN IRELAND. A Real Paddy.
THE ADVENTURES OF JOHNNY NEWCOMBE IN THE NAVY. Alfred Burton.
THE OLD ENGLISH SQUIRE. John Careless.
THE ENGLISH SPY. Bernard Blackmantle. *Two Volumes.* 7s. net.

WITH PLAIN ILLUSTRATIONS.

THE GRAVE: A Poem. Robert Blair.
ILLUSTRATIONS OF THE BOOK OF JOB. Invented and engraved by William Blake.
WINDSOR CASTLE. W. Harrison Ainsworth.
THE TOWER OF LONDON. W. Harrison Ainsworth.

FRANK FAIRLEGH. F. E. Smedley.
HANDY ANDY. Samuel Lover.
THE COMPLEAT ANGLER. Izaak Walton and Charles Cotton.
THE PICKWICK PAPERS. Charles Dickens.

Leaders of Religion.

Edited by H. C. BEECHING. With Portraits.

Crown 8vo. 2s. net each volume.

CARDINAL NEWMAN. R. H. Hutton.
JOHN WESLEY. J. H. Overton.
BISHOP WILBERFORCE. G. W. Daniell.
CARDINAL MANNING. A. W. Hutton.
CHARLES SIMEON. H. C. G. Moule.
JOHN KNOX. F. MacCunn. *Second Edition.*
JOHN HOWE. R. F. Horton.
THOMAS KEN. F. A. Clarke.
GEORGE FOX, THE QUAKER. T. Hodgkin. *Third Edition.*
JOHN KEBLE. Walter Lock.

THOMAS CHALMERS. Mrs. Oliphant. *Second Edition.*
LANCELOT ANDREWES. R. L. Ottley. *Second Edition.*
AUGUSTINE OF CANTERBURY. E. L. Cutts.
WILLIAM LAUD. W. H. Hutton. *Third Ed.*
JOHN DONNE. Augustus Jessop.
THOMAS CRANMER. A. J. Mason.
BISHOP LATIMER. R. M. Carlyle and A. J. Carlyle.
BISHOP BUTLER. W. A. Spooner.

The Library of Devotion.

With Introductions and (where necessary) Notes.

Small Pott 8vo, cloth, 2s.; leather, 2s. 6d. net each volume.

THE CONFESSIONS OF ST. AUGUSTINE. *Seventh Edition.*
THE IMITATION OF CHRIST. *Sixth Edition.*
THE CHRISTIAN YEAR. *Fifth Edition.*
LYRA INNOCENTIUM. *Second Edition.*
THE TEMPLE. *Second Edition.*
A BOOK OF DEVOTIONS. *Second Edition.*
A SERIOUS CALL TO A DEVOUT AND HOLY LIFE. *Fourth Edition.*
A GUIDE TO ETERNITY.
THE INNER WAY. *Second Edition.*
ON THE LOVE OF GOD.
THE PSALMS OF DAVID.
LYRA APOSTOLICA.
THE SONG OF SONGS.
THE THOUGHTS OF PASCAL. *Second Edition.*
A MANUAL OF CONSOLATION FROM THE SAINTS AND FATHERS.
DEVOTIONS FROM THE APOCRYPHA.
THE SPIRITUAL COMBAT.
THE DEVOTIONS OF ST. ANSELM.
BISHOP WILSON'S SACRA PRIVATA.

GRACE ABOUNDING TO THE CHIEF OF SINNERS.
LYRA SACRA: A Book of Sacred Verse. *Second Edition.*
A DAY BOOK FROM THE SAINTS AND FATHERS.
A LITTLE BOOK OF HEAVENLY WISDOM. A Selection from the English Mystics.
LIGHT, LIFE, and LOVE. A Selection from the German Mystics.
AN INTRODUCTION TO THE DEVOUT LIFE.
THE LITTLE FLOWERS OF THE GLORIOUS MESSER ST. FRANCIS AND OF HIS FRIARS.
DEATH AND IMMORTALITY.
THE SPIRITUAL GUIDE. *Second Edition.*
DEVOTIONS FOR EVERY DAY IN THE WEEK AND THE GREAT FESTIVALS.
PRECES PRIVATÆ.
HORÆ MYSTICÆ: A Day Book from the Writings of Mystics of Many Nations.

Little Books on Art.

With many Illustrations. Demy 16mo. 2s. 6d. net each volume.

Each volume consists of about 200 pages, and contains from 30 to 40 Illustrations, including a Frontispiece in Photogravure.

ALBRECHT DÜRER. J. Allen.
ARTS OF JAPAN, THE. E. Dillon. *Third Edition.*
BOOKPLATES. E. Almack.
BOTTICELLI. Mary L. Bonnor.
BURNE-JONES. F. de Lisle.
CHRISTIAN SYMBOLISM. Mrs. H. Jenner.
CHRIST IN ART. Mrs. H. Jenner.
CLAUDE. E. Dillon.
CONSTABLE. H. W. Tompkins. *Second Edition.*
COROT. A. Pollard and E. Birnstingl.
ENAMELS. Mrs. N. Dawson. *Second Edition.*
FREDERIC LEIGHTON. A. Corkran.
GEORGE ROMNEY. G. Paston.
GREEK ART. H. B. Walters. *Fourth Edition.*
GREUZE AND BOUCHER. E. F. Pollard.

HOLBEIN. Mrs. G. Fortescue.
ILLUMINATED MANUSCRIPTS. J. W. Bradley.
JEWELLERY. C. Davenport.
JOHN HOPPNER. H. P. K. Skipton.
SIR JOSHUA REYNOLDS. J. Sime. *Second Edition.*
MILLET. N. Peacock.
MINIATURES. C. Davenport.
OUR LADY IN ART. Mrs. H. Jenner.
RAPHAEL. A. R. Dryhurst.
REMBRANDT. Mrs. E. A. Sharp.
TURNER. F. Tyrrell-Gill.
VANDYCK. M. G. Smallwood.
VELASQUEZ. W. Wilberforce and A. R. Gilbert.
WATTS. R. E. D. Sketchley.

The Little Galleries.

Demy 16mo. 2s. 6d. net each volume.

Each volume contains 20 plates in Photogravure, together with a short outline of the life and work of the master to whom the book is devoted.

A LITTLE GALLERY OF REYNOLDS.
A LITTLE GALLERY OF ROMNEY.
A LITTLE GALLERY OF HOPPNER.

A LITTLE GALLERY OF MILLAIS.
A LITTLE GALLERY OF ENGLISH POETS.

The Little Guides.

With many Illustrations by E. H. NEW and other artists, and from photographs.

Small Pott 8vo, cloth, 2s. 6d. net; leather, 3s. 6d. net, each volume.

The main features of these Guides are (1) a handy and charming form; (2) illustrations from photographs and by well-known artists; (3) good plans and maps; (4) an adequate but compact presentation of everything that is interesting in the natural features, history, archæology, and architecture of the town or district treated.

CAMBRIDGE AND ITS COLLEGES. A. H. Thompson. *Third Edition, Revised.*
CHANNEL ISLANDS, THE. E. E. Bicknell.
ENGLISH LAKES, THE. F. G. Brabant.
ISLE OF WIGHT, THE. G. Clinch.
MALVERN COUNTRY, THE. B. C. A. Windle.
NORTH WALES. A. T. Story.
OXFORD AND ITS COLLEGES. J. Wells. *Ninth Edition.*

SHAKESPEARE'S COUNTRY. B. C. A. Windle. *Fourth Edition.*
ST. PAUL'S CATHEDRAL. G. Clinch.
WESTMINSTER ABBEY. G. E. Troutbeck. *Second Edition.*

BERKSHIRE. F. G. Brabant.
BUCKINGHAMSHIRE. E. S. Roscoe.
CHESHIRE. W. M. Gallichan.

METHUEN AND COMPANY LIMITED

THE LITTLE GUIDES—*continued.*

CORNWALL. A. L. Salmon.
DERBYSHIRE. J. C. Cox.
DEVON. S. Baring-Gould. *Second Edition.*
DORSET. F. R. Heath. *Second Edition.*
ESSEX. J. C. Cox.
HAMPSHIRE. J. C. Cox.
HERTFORDSHIRE. H. W. Tompkins.
KENT. G. Clinch.
KERRY. C. P. Crane.
MIDDLESEX. J. B. Firth.
MONMOUTHSHIRE. G. W. Wade and J. H. Wade.
NORFOLK. W. A. Dutt. *Second Edition, Revised.*
NORTHAMPTONSHIRE. W. Dry. *Second Ed.*
NORTHUMBERLAND. J. E. Morris.
NOTTINGHAMSHIRE. L. Guilford.
OXFORDSHIRE. F. G. Brabant.

SOMERSET. G. W. and J. H. Wade.
STAFFORDSHIRE. C. E. Masefield.
SUFFOLK. W. A. Dutt.
SURREY. J. C. Cox.
SUSSEX. F. G. Brabant. *Third Edition.*
WILTSHIRE. F. R. Heath.
YORKSHIRE, THE EAST RIDING. J. E. Morris.
YORKSHIRE, THE NORTH RIDING. J. E. Morris.
YORKSHIRE, THE WEST RIDING. J. E. Morris. *Cloth,* 3s. 6d. *net; leather,* 4s. 6d. *net.*

BRITTANY. S. Baring-Gould.
NORMANDY. C. Scudamore.
ROME. C. G. Ellaby.
SICILY. F. H. Jackson.

The Little Library.

With Introductions, Notes, and Photogravure Frontispieces.

Small Pott 8vo. Each Volume, cloth, 1s. 6d. *net.*

Anon. A LITTLE BOOK OF ENGLISH LYRICS. *Second Edition.*

Austen (Jane). PRIDE AND PREJUDICE. *Two Volumes.*
NORTHANGER ABBEY.

Bacon (Francis). THE ESSAYS OF LORD BACON.

Barham (R. H.). THE INGOLDSBY LEGENDS. *Two Volumes.*

Barnet (Annie). A LITTLE BOOK OF ENGLISH PROSE.

Beckford (William). THE HISTORY OF THE CALIPH VATHEK.

Blake (William). SELECTIONS FROM THE WORKS OF WILLIAM BLAKE.

Borrow (George). LAVENGRO. *Two Volumes.*
THE ROMANY RYE.

Browning (Robert). SELECTIONS FROM THE EARLY POEMS OF ROBERT BROWNING.

Canning (George). SELECTIONS FROM THE ANTI-JACOBIN: with GEORGE CANNING's additional Poems.

Cowley (Abraham). THE ESSAYS OF ABRAHAM COWLEY.

Crabbe (George). SELECTIONS FROM THE POEMS OF GEORGE CRABBE.

Craik (Mrs.). JOHN HALIFAX, GENTLEMAN. *Two Volumes.*

Crashaw (Richard). THE ENGLISH POEMS OF RICHARD CRASHAW.

Dante Alighieri. THE INFERNO OF DANTE. Translated by H. F. CARY.
THE PURGATORIO OF DANTE. Translated by H. F. CARY.
THE PARADISO OF DANTE. Translated by H. F. CARY.

Darley (George). SELECTIONS FROM THE POEMS OF GEORGE DARLEY.

Deane (A. C.). A LITTLE BOOK OF LIGHT VERSE.

Dickens (Charles). CHRISTMAS BOOKS. *Two Volumes.*

Ferrier (Susan). MARRIAGE. *Two Volumes.*
THE INHERITANCE. *Two Volumes.*

Gaskell (Mrs.). CRANFORD. *Second Ed.*

Hawthorne (Nathaniel). THE SCARLET LETTER.

Henderson (T. F.). A LITTLE BOOK OF SCOTTISH VERSE.

Keats (John). POEMS.

Kinglake (A. W.). EOTHEN. *Second Edition.*

General Literature

The Little Library—continued.

Lamb (Charles). ELIA, AND THE LAST ESSAYS OF ELIA.

Locker (F.). LONDON LYRICS.

Longfellow (H. W.). SELECTIONS FROM THE POEMS OF H. W. LONGFELLOW.

Marvell (Andrew). THE POEMS OF ANDREW MARVELL.

Milton (John). THE MINOR POEMS OF JOHN MILTON.

Moir (D. M.). MANSIE WAUCH.

Nichols (J. B. B.). A LITTLE BOOK OF ENGLISH SONNETS.

Rochefoucauld (La). THE MAXIMS OF LA ROCHEFOUCAULD.

Smith (Horace and James). REJECTED ADDRESSES.

Sterne (Laurence). A SENTIMENTAL JOURNEY.

Tennyson (Alfred, Lord). THE EARLY POEMS OF ALFRED, LORD TENNYSON.
IN MEMORIAM.
THE PRINCESS.
MAUD.

Thackeray (W. M.). VANITY FAIR. *Three Volumes.*
PENDENNIS. *Three Volumes.*
ESMOND.
CHRISTMAS BOOKS.

Vaughan (Henry). THE POEMS OF HENRY VAUGHAN.

Walton (Izaak). THE COMPLEAT ANGLER.

Waterhouse (Elizabeth). A LITTLE BOOK OF LIFE AND DEATH. *Thirteenth Edition.*

Wordsworth (W.). SELECTIONS FROM THE POEMS OF WILLIAM WORDSWORTH.

Wordsworth (W.) and Coleridge (S. T.). LYRICAL BALLADS. *Second Edition.*

The Little Quarto Shakespeare.

Edited by W. J. CRAIG. With Introductions and Notes.
Pott 16mo. In 40 Volumes. Leather, price 1s. net each volume.
Mahogany Revolving Book Case. 10s. net.

Miniature Library.

EUPHRANOR: A Dialogue on Youth. Edward FitzGerald. *Demy 32mo. Leather, 2s. net.*

THE LIFE OF EDWARD, LORD HERBERT OF CHERBURY. Written by himself. *Demy 32mo. Leather, 2s. net.*

POLONIUS: or Wise Saws and Modern Instances. Edward FitzGerald. *Demy 32mo. Leather, 2s. net.*

THE RUBÁIYÁT OF OMAR KHAYYÁM. Edward FitzGerald. *Fourth Edition. Leather, 1s. net.*

The New Library of Medicine.

Edited by C. W. SALEEBY. *Demy 8vo.*

CARE OF THE BODY, THE. F. Cavanagh. *Second Edition.* 7s. 6d. net.

CHILDREN OF THE NATION, THE. The Right Hon. Sir John Gorst. *Second Edition.* 7s. 6d. net.

CONTROL OF A SCOURGE, THE; or, How Cancer is Curable. Chas. P. Childe. 7s. 6d. net.

DISEASES OF OCCUPATION. Sir Thomas Oliver. 10s. 6d. net. *Second Edition.*

DRINK PROBLEM, THE, in its Medico-Sociological Aspects. Edited by T. N. Kelynack. 7s. 6d. net.

DRUGS AND THE DRUG HABIT. H. Sainsbury.

FUNCTIONAL NERVE DISEASES. A. T. Schofield. 7s. 6d. net.

HYGIENE OF MIND, THE. T. S. Clouston. *Fifth Edition.* 7s. 6d. net.

INFANT MORTALITY. Sir George Newman. 7s. 6d. net.

PREVENTION OF TUBERCULOSIS (CONSUMPTION), THE. Arthur Newsholme. 10s. 6d. net. *Second Edition.*

AIR AND HEALTH. Ronald C. Macfie. 7s. 6d. net. *Second Edition.*

The New Library of Music.

Edited by ERNEST NEWMAN. *Illustrated. Demy 8vo. 7s. 6d. net.*

BRAHMS. J. A. Fuller-Maitland. *Second Edition.*
HANDEL. R. A. Streatfeild. *Second Edition*
HUGO WOLF. Ernest Newman.

Oxford Biographies.

Illustrated. Fcap. 8vo. Each volume, cloth, 2s. 6d. net; leather, 3s. 6d. net.

DANTE ALIGHIERI. Paget Toynbee. *Third Edition.*
GIROLAMO SAVONAROLA. E. L. S. Horsburgh. *Fourth Edition.*
JOHN HOWARD. E. C. S. Gibson.
ALFRED TENNYSON. A. C. Benson. *Second Edition.*
SIR WALTER RALEIGH. I. A. Taylor.
ERASMUS. E. F. H. Capey.
THE YOUNG PRETENDER. C. S. Terry.
ROBERT BURNS. T. F. Henderson.
CHATHAM. A. S. M'Dowall.
FRANCIS OF ASSISI. Anna M. Stoddart.
CANNING. W. Alison Phillips.
BEACONSFIELD. Walter Sichel.
JOHANN WOLFGANG GOETHE. H. G. Atkins.
FRANÇOIS FÉNELON. Viscount St. Cyres.

Romantic History.

Edited by MARTIN HUME. *Illustrated. Demy 8vo.*

A series of attractive volumes in which the periods and personalities selected are such as afford romantic human interest, in addition to their historical importance.

THE FIRST GOVERNESS OF THE NETHERLANDS, MARGARET OF AUSTRIA. Eleanor E. Tremayne. 10s. 6d. net.
TWO ENGLISH QUEENS AND PHILIP. Martin Hume. 15s. net.
THE NINE DAYS' QUEEN. Richard Davey. With a Preface by Martin Hume. *Second Edition.* 10s. 6d. net.

The States of Italy.

Edited by E. ARMSTRONG and R. LANGTON DOUGLAS.

Illustrated. Demy 8vo.

A HISTORY OF MILAN UNDER THE SFORZA. Cecilia M. Ady. 10s. 6d. net.
A HISTORY OF PERUGIA. W. Heywood. 12s. 6d. net.
A HISTORY OF VERONA. A. M. Allen. 12s. 6d. net.

The Westminster Commentaries.

General Editor, WALTER LOCK.

THE ACTS OF THE APOSTLES. Edited by R. B. Rackham. *Demy 8vo. Fifth Edition.* 10s. 6d.

THE FIRST EPISTLE OF PAUL THE APOSTLE TO THE CORINTHIANS. Edited by H. L. Goudge. *Third Edition. Demy 8vo.* 6s.

THE BOOK OF EXODUS. Edited by A. H. M'Neile. With a Map and 3 Plans. *Demy 8vo.* 10s. 6d.

THE BOOK OF EZEKIEL. Edited by H. A. Redpath. *Demy 8vo.* 10s. 6d.

THE BOOK OF GENESIS. Edited with Introduction and Notes by S. R. Driver. *Eighth Edition. Demy 8vo.* 10s. 6d.

THE BOOK OF THE PROPHET ISAIAH. Edited by G. W. Wade. *Demy 8vo.* 10s. 6d.

ADDITIONS AND CORRECTIONS IN THE SEVENTH EDITION OF THE BOOK OF GENESIS. S. R. Driver. *Demy 8vo.* 1s.

THE BOOK OF JOB. Edited by E. C. S. Gibson. *Second Edition. Demy 8vo.* 6s.

THE EPISTLE OF ST. JAMES. Edited with Introduction and Notes by R. J. Knowling. *Second Edition. Demy 8vo.* 6s.

Methuen's Shilling Library.

Fcap. 8vo.

DE PROFUNDIS. Oscar Wilde.

THE LORE OF THE HONEY-BEE. Tickner Edwardes.

LETTERS FROM A SELF-MADE MERCHANT TO HIS SON. George Horace Lorimer.

SELECTED POEMS. Oscar Wilde.

THE LIFE OF ROBERT LOUIS STEVENSON. Graham Balfour.

THE LIFE OF JOHN RUSKIN. W. G. Collingwood.

THE CONDITION OF ENGLAND. G. F. G. Masterman.

PART III.—A SELECTION OF WORKS OF FICTION

Albanesi (E. Maria). SUSANNAH AND ONE OTHER. *Fourth Edition. Cr. 8vo.* 6s.

LOVE AND LOUISA. *Second Edition. Cr. 8vo.* 6s.

THE BROWN EYES OF MARY. *Third Edition. Cr. 8vo.* 6s.

I KNOW A MAIDEN. *Third Edition. Cr. 8vo.* 6s.

THE INVINCIBLE AMELIA; OR, THE POLITE ADVENTURESS. *Third Edition. Cr. 8vo.* 3s. 6d.

THE GLAD HEART. *Fifth Edition. Cr. 8vo.* 6s.

Bagot (Richard). A ROMAN MYSTERY. *Third Edition. Cr. 8vo.* 6s.

THE PASSPORT. *Fourth Edition. Cr. 8vo.* 6s.

ANTHONY CUTHBERT. *Fourth Edition. Cr. 8vo.* 6s.

LOVE'S PROXY. *Cr. 8vo.* 6s.

DONNA DIANA. *Second Edition. Cr. 8vo.* 6s.

CASTING OF NETS. *Twelfth Edition. Cr. 8vo.* 6s.

THE HOUSE OF SERRAVALLE. *Third Edition. Cr. 8vo.* 6s.

Bailey (H. C.). STORM AND TREASURE. *Third Edition. Cr. 8vo.* 6s.

THE LONELY QUEEN. *Third Edition. Cr. 8vo.* 6s.

Baring-Gould (S.). IN THE ROAR OF THE SEA. *Eighth Edition. Cr. 8vo.* 6s.

MARGERY OF QUETHER. *Second Edition. Cr. 8vo.* 6s.

THE QUEEN OF LOVE. *Fifth Edition. Cr. 8vo.* 6s.

JACQUETTA. *Third Edition. Cr. 8vo.* 6s.

KITTY ALONE. *Fifth Edition. Cr. 8vo.* 6s.

NOÉMI. Illustrated. *Fourth Edition. Cr. 8vo.* 6s.

THE BROOM-SQUIRE. Illustrated. *Fifth Edition. Cr. 8vo.* 6s.

DARTMOOR IDYLLS. *Cr. 8vo.* 6s.

GUAVAS THE TINNER. Illustrated. *Second Edition. Cr. 8vo.* 6s.

BLADYS OF THE STEWPONEY. Illustrated. *Second Edition. Cr. 8vo.* 6s.

PABO THE PRIEST. *Cr. 8vo.* 6s.

WINEFRED. Illustrated. *Second Edition. Cr. 8vo.* 6s.

ROYAL GEORGIE. Illustrated. *Cr. 8vo.* 6s.

CHRIS OF ALL SORTS. Cr. 8vo. 6s.
IN DEWISLAND. Second Edition. Cr. 8vo. 6s.
THE FROBISHERS. Cr. 8vo. 6s.
MRS. CURGENVEN OF CURGENVEN. Fifth Edition. Cr. 8vo. 6s.

Barr (Robert). IN THE MIDST OF ALARMS. Third Edition. Cr. 8vo. 6s.
THE COUNTESS TEKLA. Fifth Edition. Cr. 8vo. 6s.
THE MUTABLE MANY. Third Edition. Cr. 8vo. 6s.

Begbie (Harold). THE CURIOUS AND DIVERTING ADVENTURES OF SIR JOHN SPARROW, Bart.; or, The Progress of an Open Mind. Second Edition. Cr. 8vo. 6s.

Belloc (H.). EMMANUEL BURDEN, MERCHANT. Illustrated. Second Edition. Cr. 8vo. 6s.
A CHANGE IN THE CABINET. Third Edition. Cr. 8vo. 6s.

Bennett (Arnold). CLAYHANGER. Tenth Edition. Cr. 8vo. 6s.
THE CARD. Sixth Edition. Cr. 8vo. 6s.
HILDA LESSWAYS. Seventh Edition. Cr. 8vo. 6s.

Benson (E. F.). DODO: A Detail of the Day. Sixteenth Edition. Cr. 8vo. 6s.

Birmingham (George A.). SPANISH GOLD. Sixth Edition. Cr. 8vo. 6s.
THE SEARCH PARTY. Fifth Edition. Cr. 8vo. 6s.
LALAGE'S LOVERS. Third Edition. Cr. 8vo. 6s.
*THE ADVENTURES OF DR. WHITTY. Cr. 8vo. 6s.

Bowen (Marjorie). I WILL MAINTAIN. Seventh Edition. Cr. 8vo. 6s.
DEFENDER OF THE FAITH. Fourth Edition. Cr. 8vo. 6s.

Castle (Agnes and Egerton). FLOWER O' THE ORANGE, and Other Tales. Third Edition. Cr. 8vo. 6s.

Clifford (Mrs. W. K.). THE GETTING WELL OF DOROTHY. Illustrated. Second Edition. Cr. 8vo. 3s. 6d.

Conrad (Joseph). THE SECRET AGENT: A Simple Tale. Fourth Ed. Cr. 8vo. 6s.
A SET OF SIX. Fourth Edition. Cr. 8vo. 6s.
UNDER WESTERN EYES. Second Ed. Cr. 8vo. 6s.

Corelli (Marie). A ROMANCE OF TWO WORLDS. Thirty-first Ed. Cr. 8vo. 6s.
VENDETTA. Twenty-ninth Edition. Cr. 8vo. 6s.
THELMA: A Norwegian Princess. Forty-second Edition. Cr. 8vo. 6s.
ARDATH: The Story of a Dead Self. Twentieth Edition. Cr. 8vo. 6s.

THE SOUL OF LILITH. Seventeenth Edition. Cr. 8vo. 6s.
WORMWOOD: A Drama of Paris. Eighteenth Edition. Cr. 8vo. 6s.
BARABBAS: A Dream of the World's Tragedy. Forty-fifth Edition. Cr. 8vo. 6s.
THE SORROWS OF SATAN. Fifty-seventh Edition. Cr. 8vo. 6s.
THE MASTER CHRISTIAN. Thirteenth Edition. 179th Thousand. Cr. 8vo. 6s.
TEMPORAL POWER: A Study in Supremacy. Second Edition. 150th Thousand. Cr. 8vo. 6s.
GOD'S GOOD MAN: A Simple Love Story. Fifteenth Edition. 154th Thousand. Cr. 8vo. 6s.
HOLY ORDERS: the Tragedy of a Quiet Life. Second Edition. 120th Thousand. Crown 8vo. 6s.
THE MIGHTY ATOM. Twenty-ninth Edition. Cr. 8vo. 6s.
BOY: a Sketch. Twelfth Edition. Cr. 8vo. 6s.
CAMEOS. Fourteenth Edition. Cr. 8vo. 6s.
THE LIFE EVERLASTING. Fifth Ed. Cr. 8vo. 6s.

Crockett (S. R.). LOCHINVAR. Illustrated. Third Edition. Cr. 8vo. 6s.
THE STANDARD BEARER. Second Edition. Cr. 8vo. 6s.

Croker (B. M.). THE OLD CANTONMENT. Second Edition. Cr. 8vo. 6s.
JOHANNA. Second Edition. Cr. 8vo. 6s.
THE HAPPY VALLEY. Fourth Edition. Cr. 8vo. 6s.
A NINE DAYS' WONDER. Fourth Edition. Cr. 8vo. 6s.
PEGGY OF THE BARTONS. Seventh Edition. Cr. 8vo. 6s.
ANGEL. Fifth Edition. Cr. 8vo. 6s.
KATHERINE THE ARROGANT. Sixth Edition. Cr. 8vo. 6s.
BABES IN THE WOOD. Fourth Edition. Cr. 8vo. 6s.

Doyle (A. Conan). ROUND THE RED LAMP. Twelfth Edition. Cr. 8vo. 6s.

Duncan (Sara Jeannette) (Mrs. Everard Cotes). A VOYAGE OF CONSOLATION. Illustrated. Third Edition. Cr. 8vo. 6s.
COUSIN CINDERELLA. Second Edition. Cr. 8vo. 6s.
THE BURNT OFFERING. Second Edition. Cr. 8vo. 6s.

Fenn (G. Manville). SYD BELTON: The Boy who would not go to Sea. Illustrated. Second Ed. Cr. 8vo. 3s. 6d.

Findlater (J. H.). THE GREEN GRAVES OF BALGOWRIE. Fifth Edition. Cr. 8vo. 6s.
THE LADDER TO THE STARS. Second Edition. Cr. 8vo. 6s.

FICTION

Findlater (Mary). A NARROW WAY. *Third Edition. Cr. 8vo. 6s.*
OVER THE HILLS. *Second Edition. Cr. 8vo. 6s.*
THE ROSE OF JOY. *Third Edition. Cr. 8vo. 6s.*
A BLIND BIRD'S NEST. Illustrated. *Second Edition. Cr. 8vo. 6s.*

Fry (B. and C. B.). A MOTHER'S SON. *Fifth Edition. Cr. 8vo. 6s.*

Gibbon (Perceval). MARGARET HARDING. *Third Edition. Cr. 8vo. 6s.*

Gissing (George). THE CROWN OF LIFE. *Cr. 8vo. 6s.*

Harraden (Beatrice). IN VARYING MOODS. *Fourteenth Edition. Cr. 8vo. 6s.*
HILDA STRAFFORD and THE REMITTANCE MAN. *Twelfth Ed. Cr. 8vo. 6s.*
INTERPLAY. *Fifth Edition. Cr. 8vo. 6s.*

Hichens (Robert). THE PROPHET OF BERKELEY SQUARE. *Second Edition. Cr. 8vo. 6s.*
TONGUES OF CONSCIENCE. *Third Edition. Cr. 8vo. 6s.*
FELIX. *Eighth and Cheaper Edition. Cr. 8vo. 2s. net.*
THE WOMAN WITH THE FAN. *Eighth Edition. Cr. 8vo. 6s.*
BYEWAYS. *Cr. 8vo. 6s.*
THE GARDEN OF ALLAH. *Twenty-first Edition. Cr. 8vo. 6s.*
THE BLACK SPANIEL. *Cr. 8vo. 6s.*
THE CALL OF THE BLOOD. *Seventh Edition. Cr. 8vo. 6s.*
BARBARY SHEEP. *Second Edition. Cr. 8vo. 6s.*
THE DWELLER ON THE THRESHOLD. *Cr. 8vo. 6s.*

Hope (Anthony). THE GOD IN THE CAR. *Eleventh Edition. Cr. 8vo. 6s.*
A CHANGE OF AIR. *Sixth Edition. Cr. 8vo. 6s.*
A MAN OF MARK. *Seventh Ed. Cr. 8vo. 6s.*
THE CHRONICLES OF COUNT ANTONIO. *Sixth Edition. Cr. 8vo. 6s.*
PHROSO. Illustrated. *Eighth Edition. Cr. 8vo. 6s.*
SIMON DALE. Illustrated. *Eighth Edition. Cr. 8vo. 6s.*
THE KING'S MIRROR. *Fifth Edition. Cr. 8vo. 6s.*
QUISANTE. *Fourth Edition. Cr. 8vo. 6s.*
THE DOLLY DIALOGUES. *Cr. 8vo. 6s.*
A SERVANT OF THE PUBLIC. Illustrated. *Fourth Edition. Cr. 8vo. 6s.*
TALES OF TWO PEOPLE. *Third Edition. Cr. 8vo. 6s.*
THE GREAT MISS DRIVER. *Fourth Edition. Cr. 8vo. 6s.*
MRS. MAXON PROTESTS. *Third Edition. Cr. 8vo. 6s.*

Hutten (Baroness von). THE HALO. *Fifth Edition. Cr. 8vo. 6s.*

Hyne (C. J. Cutcliffe). MR. HORROCKS, PURSER. *Fifth Edition. Cr. 8vo. 6s.*

'Inner Shrine' (Author of the). THE WILD OLIVE. *Third Edition. Cr. 8vo. 6s.*

Jacobs (W. W.). MANY CARGOES. *Thirty-second Edition. Cr. 8vo. 3s. 6d.*
SEA URCHINS. *Sixteenth Edition. Cr. 8vo. 3s. 6d.*
A MASTER OF CRAFT. Illustrated. *Ninth Edition. Cr. 8vo. 3s. 6d.*
LIGHT FREIGHTS. Illustrated. *Eighth Edition. Cr. 8vo. 3s. 6d.*
THE SKIPPER'S WOOING. *Eleventh Edition. Cr. 8vo. 3s. 6d.*
AT SUNWICH PORT. Illustrated. *Tenth Edition. Cr. 8vo. 3s. 6d.*
DIALSTONE LANE. Illustrated. *Eighth Edition. Cr. 8vo. 3s. 6d.*
ODD CRAFT. Illustrated. *Fourth Edition. Cr. 8vo. 3s. 6d.*
THE LADY OF THE BARGE. Illustrated. *Ninth Edition. Cr. 8vo. 3s. 6d.*
SALTHAVEN. Illustrated. *Third Edition. Cr. 8vo. 3s. 6d.*
SAILORS' KNOTS. Illustrated. *Fifth Edition. Cr. 8vo. 3s. 6d.*
SHORT CRUISES. *Third Edition. Cr. 8vo. 3s. 6d.*

James (Henry). THE GOLDEN BOWL. *Third Edition. Cr. 8vo. 6s.*
THE FINER GRAIN. *Third Edition. Cr. 8vo. 6s.*

Le Queux (William). THE HUNCHBACK OF WESTMINSTER. *Third Edition. Cr. 8vo. 6s.*
THE CLOSED BOOK. *Third Edition. Cr. 8vo. 6s.*
THE VALLEY OF THE SHADOW. Illustrated. *Third Edition. Cr. 8vo. 6s.*
BEHIND THE THRONE. *Third Edition. Cr. 8vo. 6s.*

London (Jack). WHITE FANG. *Eighth Edition. Cr. 8vo. 6s.*

Lucas (E. V.). LISTENER'S LURE; An Oblique Narration. *Eighth Edition. Fcap. 8vo. 5s.*
OVER BEMERTON'S: An Easy-going Chronicle. *Ninth Edition. Fcap 8vo. 5s.*
MR. INGLESIDE. *Eighth Edition. Cr. 8vo. 6s.*

Lyall (Edna). DERRICK VAUGHAN, NOVELIST. *44th Thousand. Cr. 8vo. 3s. 6d.*

Macnaughtan (S.). THE FORTUNE OF CHRISTINA M'NAB. *Fifth Edition. Cr. 8vo. 6s.*
PETER AND JANE. *Fourth Edition. Cr. 8vo. 6s.*

Malet (Lucas). COLONEL ENDERBY'S WIFE. *Fifth Edition. Cr. 8vo. 6s.*
A COUNSEL OF PERFECTION. *Second Edition. Cr. 8vo. 6s.*
THE WAGES OF SIN. *Sixteenth Edition. Cr. 8vo. 6s.*
THE CARISSIMA. *Fifth Ed. Cr. 8vo. 6s.*
THE GATELESS BARRIER. *Fifth Edition. Cr. 8vo. 6s.*
THE HISTORY OF SIR RICHARD CALMADY. *Ninth Edition. Cr. 8vo. 2s. net.*

Mann (Mrs. M. E.). THE PARISH NURSE. *Fourth Edition. Cr. 8vo. 6s.*
A SHEAF OF CORN. *Second Edition. Cr. 8vo. 6s.*
THE HEART-SMITER. *Second Edition. Cr. 8vo. 6s.*
AVENGING CHILDREN. *Second Edition. Cr. 8vo. 6s.*
ASTRAY IN ARCADY. *Second Edition. Cr. 8vo. 6s.*
THERE WAS A WIDOW. *Second Edition. Cr. 8vo. 6s.*

Marsh (Richard). THE COWARD BEHIND THE CURTAIN. *Cr. 8vo. 6s.*
THE SURPRISING HUSBAND. *Second Edition. Cr. 8vo. 6s.*
LIVE MEN'S SHOES. *Second Edition. Cr. 8vo. 6s.*

Marshall (Archibald). MANY JUNES. *Second Edition. Cr. 8vo. 6s.*
THE SQUIRE'S DAUGHTER. *Third Edition. Cr. 8vo. 6s.*
THE ELDEST SON. *Third Edition. Cr. 8vo. 6s.*

Mason (A. E. W.). CLEMENTINA. Illustrated. *Seventh Edition. Cr. 8vo. 2s. net.*

Maxwell (W. B.). VIVIEN. *Tenth Edition. Cr. 8vo. 6s.*
THE RAGGED MESSENGER. *Third Edition. Cr. 8vo. 6s.*
FABULOUS FANCIES. *Cr. 8vo. 6s.*
THE GUARDED FLAME. *Seventh Edition. Cr. 8vo. 6s.*
ODD LENGTHS. *Second Ed. Cr. 8vo. 6s.*
HILL RISE. *Fourth Edition. Cr. 8vo. 6s.*
THE COUNTESS OF MAYBURY: BETWEEN YOU AND I. *Fourth Edition. Cr. 8vo. 6s.*
THE REST CURE. *Fourth Edition. Cr. 8vo. 6s.*

Meade (L. T.). DRIFT. *Second Edition. Cr. 8vo. 6s.*
RESURGAM. *Second Edition. Cr. 8vo. 6s.*
VICTORY. *Cr. 8vo. 6s.*
A GIRL OF THE PEOPLE. Illustrated. *Fourth Edition. Cr. 8vo. 3s. 6d.*
HEPSY GIPSY. Illustrated. *Cr. 8vo. 2s. 6d.*
THE HONOURABLE MISS: A STORY OF AN OLD-FASHIONED TOWN. Illustrated. *Second Edition. Cr. 8vo. 3s. 6d.*

Mitford (Bertram). THE SIGN OF THE SPIDER. Illustrated. *Seventh Edition. Cr. 8vo. 3s. 6d.*

Molesworth (Mrs.). THE RED GRANGE. Illustrated. *Second Edition. Cr. 8vo. 3s. 6d.*

Montague (C. E.). A HIND LET LOOSE. *Third Edition. Cr. 8vo. 6s.*

Morrison (Arthur). TALES OF MEAN STREETS. *Seventh Edition. Cr. 8vo. 6s.*
A CHILD OF THE JAGO. *Sixth Edition. Cr. 8vo. 6s.*
THE HOLE IN THE WALL. *Fourth Edition. Cr. 8vo. 6s.*
DIVERS VANITIES. *Cr. 8vo. 6s.*

Nesbit (E.), (Mrs. H. Bland). THE RED HOUSE. Illustrated. *Fifth Edition. Cr. 8vo. 6s.*
DORMANT. *Second Edition. Cr. 8vo. 6s.*

Ollivant (Alfred). OWD BOB, THE GREY DOG OF KENMUIR. With a Frontispiece. *Eleventh Ed. Cr. 8vo. 6s.*
THE TAMING OF JOHN BLUNT. *Second Edition. Cr. 8vo. 6s.*

Onions (Oliver). GOOD BOY SELDOM: A ROMANCE OF ADVERTISEMENT. *Second Edition. Cr. 8vo. 6s.*

Oppenheim (E. Phillips). MASTER OF MEN. *Fifth Edition. Cr. 8vo. 6s.*
THE MISSING DELORA. Illustrated. *Fourth Edition. Cr. 8vo. 6s.*

Orczy (Baroness). FIRE IN STUBBLE. *Third Edition. Cr. 8vo. 6s.*

Oxenham (John). A WEAVER OF WEBS. Illustrated. *Fifth Ed. Cr. 8vo. 6s.*
THE GATE OF THE DESERT. *Eighth Edition. Cr. 8vo. 2s. net.*
PROFIT AND LOSS. *Fourth Edition. Cr. 8vo. 6s.*
THE LONG ROAD. *Fourth Edition. Cr. 8vo. 6s.*
THE SONG OF HYACINTH, AND OTHER STORIES. *Second Edition. Cr. 8vo. 6s.*
MY LADY OF SHADOWS. *Fourth Edition. Cr. 8vo. 6s.*
LAURISTONS. *Fourth Edition. Cr. 8vo. 6s.*
THE COIL OF CARNE. *Sixth Edition. Cr. 8vo. 6s.*

Pain (Barry). THE EXILES OF FALOO. *Second Edition. Crown 8vo. 6s.*

Parker (Gilbert). PIERRE AND HIS PEOPLE. *Seventh Edition. Cr. 8vo. 6s.*
MRS. FALCHION. *Fifth Edition. Cr. 8vo. 6s.*
THE TRANSLATION OF A SAVAGE. *Fourth Edition. Cr. 8vo. 6s.*
THE TRAIL OF THE SWORD. Illustrated. *Tenth Edition. Cr. 8vo. 6s.*

Fiction

WHEN VALMOND CAME TO PONTIAC: The Story of a Lost Napoleon. *Seventh Edition. Cr. 8vo. 6s.*
AN ADVENTURER OF THE NORTH. The Last Adventures of 'Pretty Pierre.' *Fifth Edition. Cr. 8vo. 6s.*
THE SEATS OF THE MIGHTY. Illustrated. *Seventeenth Edition. Cr. 8vo. 6s.*
THE BATTLE OF THE STRONG: a Romance of Two Kingdoms. Illustrated. *Seventh Edition. Cr. 8vo. 6s.*
THE POMP OF THE LAVILETTES. *Third Edition. Cr. 8vo. 3s. 6d.*
NORTHERN LIGHTS. *Fourth Edition. Cr. 8vo. 6s.*

Pasture (Mrs. Henry de la). THE TYRANT. *Fourth Edition. Cr. 8vo. 6s.*

Pemberton (Max). THE FOOTSTEPS OF A THRONE. Illustrated. *Fourth Edition. Cr. 8vo. 6s.*
I CROWN THEE KING. Illustrated. *Cr. 8vo. 6s.*
LOVE THE HARVESTER: A Story of the Shires. Illustrated. *Third Edition. Cr. 8vo. 3s. 6d.*
THE MYSTERY OF THE GREEN HEART. *Third Edition. Cr. 8vo. 6s.*

Perrin (Alice). THE CHARM. *Fifth Edition. Cr. 8vo. 6s.*

Phillpotts (Eden). LYING PROPHETS. *Third Edition. Cr. 8vo. 6s.*
CHILDREN OF THE MIST. *Sixth Edition. Cr. 8vo. 6s.*
THE HUMAN BOY. With a Frontispiece. *Seventh Edition. Cr. 8vo. 6s.*
SONS OF THE MORNING. *Second Edition. Cr. 8vo. 6s.*
THE RIVER. *Fourth Edition. Cr. 8vo. 6s.*
THE AMERICAN PRISONER. *Fourth Edition. Cr. 8vo. 6s.*
THE SECRET WOMAN. *Fourth Edition. Cr. 8vo. 6s.*
KNOCK AT A VENTURE. *Third Edition. Cr. 8vo. 6s.*
THE PORTREEVE. *Fourth Edition. Cr. 8vo. 6s.*
THE POACHER'S WIFE. *Second Edition. Cr. 8vo. 6s.*
THE STRIKING HOURS. *Second Edition. Cr. 8vo. 6s.*
DEMETER'S DAUGHTER. *Third Edition. Cr. 8vo. 6s.*

Pickthall (Marmaduke). SAÏD THE FISHERMAN. *Eighth Edition. Cr. 8vo. 6s.*

'Q' (A. T. Quiller Couch). THE WHITE WOLF. *Second Edition. Cr. 8vo. 6s.*
THE MAYOR OF TROY. *Fourth Edition. Cr. 8vo. 6s.*

MERRY-GARDEN and other Stories. *Cr. 8vo. 6s.*
MAJOR VIGOUREUX. *Third Edition. Cr. 8vo. 6s.*

Ridge (W. Pett). ERB. *Second Edition. Cr. 8vo. 6s.*
A SON OF THE STATE. *Third Edition. Cr. 8vo. 3s. 6d.*
A BREAKER OF LAWS. *Cr. 8vo. 3s. 6d.*
MRS. GALER'S BUSINESS. Illustrated. *Second Edition. Cr. 8vo. 6s.*
THE WICKHAMSES. *Fourth Edition. Cr. 8vo. 6s.*
NAME OF GARLAND. *Third Edition. Cr. 8vo. 6s.*
SPLENDID BROTHER. *Fourth Edition. Cr. 8vo. 6s.*
NINE TO SIX-THIRTY. *Third Edition. Cr. 8vo. 6s.*
THANKS TO SANDERSON. *Second Edition. Cr. 8vo. 6s.*

Robins (Elizabeth). THE CONVERT. *Third Edition. Cr. 8vo. 6s.*

Russell (W. Clark). MY DANISH SWEETHEART. Illustrated. *Fifth Edition. Cr. 8vo. 6s.*
HIS ISLAND PRINCESS. Illustrated. *Second Edition. Cr. 8vo. 6s.*
ABANDONED. *Second Edition. Cr. 8vo. 6s.*
MASTER ROCKAFELLAR'S VOYAGE. Illustrated. *Fourth Edition. Cr. 8vo. 3s. 6d.*

Sidgwick (Mrs. Alfred). THE KINSMAN. Illustrated. *Third Edition. Cr. 8vo. 6s.*
THE SEVERINS. *Sixth Edition. Cr. 8vo. 6s.*
THE LANTERN-BEARERS. *Third Ed. Cr. 8vo. 6s.*
ANTHEA'S GUEST. *Fifth Edition. Cr. 8vo. 6s.*

Somerville (E. Œ.) and Ross (Martin). DAN RUSSEL THE FOX. Illustrated. *Fourth Edition. Cr. 8vo. 6s.*

Thurston (E. Temple). MIRAGE. *Fourth Edition. Cr. 8vo. 6s.*

Watson (H. B. Marriott). TWISTED EGLANTINE. Illustrated. *Third Edition. Cr. 8vo. 6s.*
THE HIGH TOBY. *Third Edition. Cr. 8vo. 6s.*
THE PRIVATEERS. Illustrated. *Second Edition. Cr. 8vo. 6s.*
ALISE OF ASTRA. *Third Edition. Cr. 8vo. 6s.*

Webling (Peggy). THE STORY OF VIRGINIA PERFECT. *Third Edition. Cr. 8vo. 6s.*
THE SPIRIT OF MIRTH. *Fifth Edition. Cr. 8vo. 6s.*

Weyman (Stanley). UNDER THE RED ROBE. Illustrated. *Twenty-third Edition. Cr. 8vo. 6s.*

Whitby (Beatrice). ROSAMUND. *Second Edition. Cr. 8vo. 6s.*

Williamson (C. N. and A. M.). THE LIGHTNING CONDUCTOR: The Strange Adventures of a Motor Car. Illustrated. *Seventeenth Edition. Cr. 8vo. 6s.* Also *Cr. 8vo. 1s. net.*
THE PRINCESS PASSES: A Romance of a Motor. Illustrated. *Ninth Edition. Cr. 8vo. 6s.*
MY FRIEND THE CHAUFFEUR. Illustrated. *Twelfth Edition. Cr. 8vo. 2s. net.*
LADY BETTY ACROSS THE WATER. *Eleventh Edition. Cr. 8vo. 6s.*
THE CAR OF DESTINY AND ITS ERRAND IN SPAIN. Illustrated. *Fifth Edition. Cr. 8vo. 6s.*
THE BOTOR CHAPERON. Illustrated. *Sixth Edition. Cr. 8vo. 6s.*
SCARLET RUNNER. Illustrated. *Third Edition. Cr. 8vo. 6s.*
SET IN SILVER. Illustrated. *Fourth Edition. Cr. 8vo. 6s.*
LORD LOVELAND DISCOVERS AMERICA. *Second Edition. Cr. 8vo. 6s.*
THE GOLDEN SILENCE. *Sixth Edition. Cr. 8vo. 6s.*
THE GUESTS OF HERCULES. *Cr. 8vo. 6s.*

Wyllarde (Dolf). THE PATHWAY OF THE PIONEER (Nous Autres). *Sixth Edition. Cr. 8vo. 6s.*
THE UNOFFICIAL HONEYMOON. *Sixth Edition. Cr. 8vo. 6s.*

Methuen's Two-Shilling Novels.

Cr. 8vo. 2s. net.

THE GATE OF THE DESERT. John Oxenham.
THE SEVERINS. Mrs. Alfred Sidgwick.
CLEMENTINA. A. E. W. Mason.
THE PRINCESS VIRGINIA. C. N. and A. M. Williamson.
COLONEL ENDERBY'S WIFE. Lucas Malet.

Books for Boys and Girls.

Illustrated. Crown 8vo. 3s. 6d.

CROSS AND DAGGER. The Crusade of the Children, 1212. W. Scott Durrant.
THE GETTING WELL OF DOROTHY. Mrs. W. K. Clifford.
ONLY A GUARD-ROOM DOG. Edith E. Cuthell.
MASTER ROCKAFELLAR'S VOYAGE. W. Clark Russell.
SYD BELTON: The Boy who would not go to Sea. G. Manville Fenn.
THE RED GRANGE. Mrs. Molesworth.
A GIRL OF THE PEOPLE. L. T. Meade.
HEPSY GIPSY. L. T. Meade. 2s. 6d.
THE HONOURABLE MISS. L. T. Meade.
THERE WAS ONCE A PRINCE. Mrs. M. E. Mann.

Methuen's Shilling Novels.

JANE. Marie Corelli.
UNDER THE RED ROBE. Stanley J. Weyman.
LADY BETTY ACROSS THE WATER. C. N. & A. M. Williamson.
MIRAGE. E. Temple Thurston.
VIRGINIA PERFECT. Peggy Webling.
SPANISH GOLD. G. A. Birmingham.
BARBARY SHEEP. Robert Hichens.

FICTION

The Novels of Alexandre Dumas.

Medium 8vo. Price 6d. Double Volumes, 1s.

ACTÉ.
THE ADVENTURES OF CAPTAIN PAMPHILE.
AMAURY.
THE BIRD OF FATE.
THE BLACK TULIP.
THE CASTLE OF EPPSTEIN.
CATHERINE BLUM.
CÉCILE.
THE CHÂTELET.
THE CHEVALIER D'HARMENTAL. (Double volume.)
CHICOT THE JESTER.
CHICOT REDIVIVUS.
THE COMTE DE MONTGOMMERY.
CONSCIENCE.
THE CONVICT'S SON.
THE CORSICAN BROTHERS; and OTHO THE ARCHER.
CROP-EARED JACQUOT.
DOM GORENFLOT.
THE DUC D'ANJOU.
THE FATAL COMBAT.
THE FENCING MASTER.
FERNANDE.
GABRIEL LAMBERT.
GEORGES.
THE GREAT MASSACRE.
HENRI DE NAVARRE.
HÉLÈNE DE CHAVERNY.
THE HOROSCOPE.
LEONE-LEONA.
LOUISE DE LA VALLIÈRE. (Double volume.)
THE MAN IN THE IRON MASK. (Double volume.)
MAÎTRE ADAM.
THE MOUTH OF HELL.
NANON. (Double volume.)
OLYMPIA.
PAULINE; PASCAL BRUNO; and BONTEKOE.
PÈRE LA RUINE.
THE PORTE SAINT-ANTOINE.
THE PRINCE OF THIEVES.
THE REMINISCENCES OF ANTONY.
ST. QUENTIN.
ROBIN HOOD.
SAMUEL GELB.
THE SNOWBALL AND THE SULTANETTA.
SYLVANDIRE.
THE TAKING OF CALAIS.
TALES OF THE SUPERNATURAL.
TALES OF STRANGE ADVENTURE.
TALES OF TERROR.
THE THREE MUSKETEERS. (Double volume.)
TOURNEY OF THE RUE ST. ANTOINE.
THE TRAGEDY OF NANTES.
TWENTY YEARS AFTER. (Double volume.)
THE WILD-DUCK SHOOTER.
THE WOLF-LEADER.

Methuen's Sixpenny Books.

Medium 8vo.

Albanesi (E. Maria). LOVE AND LOUISA.
I KNOW A MAIDEN.
THE BLUNDER OF AN INNOCENT.
PETER A PARASITE.

Anstey (F.). A BAYARD OF BENGAL.

Austen (J.). PRIDE AND PREJUDICE.

Bagot (Richard). A ROMAN MYSTERY.
CASTING OF NETS.
DONNA DIANA.

Balfour (Andrew). BY STROKE OF SWORD.

Baring-Gould (S.). FURZE BLOOM.
CHEAP JACK ZITA.
KITTY ALONE.
URITH.
THE BROOM SQUIRE.
IN THE ROAR OF THE SEA.
NOÉMI.
A BOOK OF FAIRY TALES. Illustrated.
LITTLE TU'PENNY.
WINEFRED.
THE FROBISHERS.
THE QUEEN OF LOVE.
ARMINELL.
BLADYS OF THE STEWPONEY.
CHRIS OF ALL SORTS.

Barr (Robert). JENNIE BAXTER.
IN THE MIDST OF ALARMS.
THE COUNTESS TEKLA.
THE MUTABLE MANY.

Benson (E. F.). DODO.
THE VINTAGE.

Brontë (Charlotte). SHIRLEY.

Brownell (C. L.). THE HEART OF JAPAN.

Burton (J. Bloundelle). ACROSS THE SALT SEAS.

Caffyn (Mrs.). ANNE MAULEVERER.

Capes (Bernard). THE LAKE OF WINE.
THE GREAT SKENE MYSTERY.

Clifford (Mrs. W. K.). A FLASH OF SUMMER.
MRS. KEITH'S CRIME.

Corbett (Julian). A BUSINESS IN GREAT WATERS.

Croker (Mrs. B. M.). ANGEL.
A STATE SECRET.
PEGGY OF THE BARTONS.
JOHANNA.

Dante (Alighieri). THE DIVINE COMEDY (Cary).

Doyle (A. Conan). ROUND THE RED LAMP.

Duncan (Sara Jeannette). THOSE DELIGHTFUL AMERICANS.

Eliot (George). THE MILL ON THE FLOSS.

Findlater (Jane H.). THE GREEN GRAVES OF BALGOWRIE.

Gallon (Tom). RICKERBY'S FOLLY.

Gaskell (Mrs.). CRANFORD.
MARY BARTON.
NORTH AND SOUTH.

Gerard (Dorothea). HOLY MATRIMONY.
THE CONQUEST OF LONDON.
MADE OF MONEY.

Gissing (G.). THE TOWN TRAVELLER.
THE CROWN OF LIFE.

Glanville (Ernest). THE INCA'S TREASURE.
THE KLOOF BRIDE.

Gleig (Charles). BUNTER'S CRUISE.

Grimm (The Brothers). GRIMM'S FAIRY TALES.

Hope (Anthony). A MAN OF MARK.
A CHANGE OF AIR.
THE CHRONICLES OF COUNT ANTONIO.
PHROSO.
THE DOLLY DIALOGUES.

Hornung (E. W.). DEAD MEN TELL NO TALES.

Hyne (C. J. C.). PRINCE RUPERT THE BUCCANEER.

Ingraham (J. H.). THE THRONE OF DAVID.

Le Queux (W.). THE HUNCHBACK OF WESTMINSTER.
THE CROOKED WAY.
*THE VALLEY OF THE SHADOW.

Levett-Yeats (S. K.). THE TRAITOR'S WAY.
ORRAIN.

Linton (E. Lynn). THE TRUE HISTORY OF JOSHUA DAVIDSON.

Lyall (Edna). DERRICK VAUGHAN.

Malet (Lucas). THE CARISSIMA.
A COUNSEL OF PERFECTION.

Mann (Mrs. M. E.). MRS. PETER HOWARD.
A LOST ESTATE.
THE CEDAR STAR.
ONE ANOTHER'S BURDENS.
THE PATTEN EXPERIMENT.
A WINTER'S TALE.

Marchmont (A. W.). MISER HOADLEY'S SECRET.
A MOMENT'S ERROR.

Marryat (Captain). PETER SIMPLE.
JACOB FAITHFUL.

March (Richard). A METAMORPHOSIS.
THE TWICKENHAM PEERAGE.
THE GODDESS.
THE JOSS.

FICTION

Mason (A. E. W.). CLEMENTINA.

Mathers (Helen). HONEY.
GRIFF OF GRIFFITHSCOURT.
SAM'S SWEETHEART.
THE FERRYMAN.

Meade (Mrs. L. T.). DRIFT.

Miller (Esther). LIVING LIES.

Mitford (Bertram). THE SIGN OF THE SPIDER.

Montresor (F. F.). THE ALIEN.

Morrison (Arthur). THE HOLE IN THE WALL.

Nesbit (E.). THE RED HOUSE.

Norris (W. E.). HIS GRACE.
GILES INGILBY.
THE CREDIT OF THE COUNTY.
LORD LEONARD THE LUCKLESS.
MATTHEW AUSTEN.
CLARISSA FURIOSA.

Oliphant (Mrs.). THE LADY'S WALK.
SIR ROBERT'S FORTUNE.
THE PRODIGALS.
THE TWO MARYS.

Oppenheim (E. P.). MASTER OF MEN.

Parker (Gilbert). THE POMP OF THE LAVILETTES.
WHEN VALMOND CAME TO PONTIAC.
THE TRAIL OF THE SWORD.

Pemberton (Max). THE FOOTSTEPS OF A THRONE.
I CROWN THEE KING.

Phillpotts (Eden). THE HUMAN BOY.
CHILDREN OF THE MIST.
THE POACHER'S WIFE.
THE RIVER.

'Q' (A. T. Quiller Couch). THE WHITE WOLF.

Ridge (W. Pett). A SON OF THE STATE.
LOST PROPERTY.
GEORGE and THE GENERAL.
A BREAKER OF LAWS.
ERB.

Russell (W. Clark). ABANDONED.
A MARRIAGE AT SEA.
MY DANISH SWEETHEART.
HIS ISLAND PRINCESS.

Sergeant (Adeline). THE MASTER OF BEECHWOOD.
BARBARA'S MONEY.
THE YELLOW DIAMOND.
THE LOVE THAT OVERCAME.

Sidgwick (Mrs. Alfred). THE KINSMAN.

Surtees (R. S.). HANDLEY CROSS.
MR. SPONGE'S SPORTING TOUR.
ASK MAMMA.

Walford (Mrs. L. B.). MR. SMITH.
COUSINS.
THE BABY'S GRANDMOTHER.
TROUBLESOME DAUGHTERS.

Wallace (General Lew). BEN-HUR.
THE FAIR GOD.

Watson (H. B. Marriott). THE ADVENTURERS.
CAPTAIN FORTUNE.

Weekes (A. B.). PRISONERS OF WAR.

Wells (H. G.). THE SEA LADY.

Whitby (Beatrice). THE RESULT OF AN ACCIDENT.

White (Percy). A PASSIONATE PILGRIM.

Williamson (Mrs. C. N.). PAPA.

Books for Travellers.

Crown 8vo. 6s. each.

Each volume contains a number of Illustrations in Colour.

A Wanderer in Paris. E. V. Lucas.
A Wanderer in Holland. E. V. Lucas.
A Wanderer in London. E. V. Lucas.
The Norfolk Broads. W. A. Dutt.
The New Forest. Horace G. Hutchinson.
Naples. Arthur H. Norway.
The Cities of Umbria. Edward Hutton.
The Cities of Spain. Edward Hutton.
Florence and the Cities of Northern Tuscany, with Genoa. Edward Hutton.
Rome. Edward Hutton.
Venice and Venetia. Edward Hutton.
The Bretons at Home. F. M. Gostling.
The Land of Pardons (Brittany). Anatole Le Braz.
A Book of the Rhine. S. Baring-Gould.
The Naples Riviera. H. M. Vaughan.
Days in Cornwall. C. Lewis Hind.
Through East Anglia in a Motor Car. J. E. Vincent.
The Skirts of the Great City. Mrs. G. Bell.
Round about Wiltshire. A. G. Bradley.
Scotland of To-day. T. F. Henderson and Francis Watt.
Norway and its Fjords. M. A. Wyllie.

Some Books on Art.

Art and Life. T. Sturge Moore. Illustrated. *Cr. 8vo. 5s. net.*
Aims and Ideals in Art. George Clausen. Illustrated. *Second Edition. Large Post 8vo. 5s. net.*
Six Lectures on Painting. George Clausen. Illustrated. *Third Edition. Large Post 8vo. 3s. 6d. net.*
Francesco Guardi, 1712-1793. G. A. Simonson. Illustrated. *Imperial 4to. £2 2s. net.*
Illustrations of the Book of Job. William Blake. *Quarto. £1 1s. net.*
John Lucas, Portrait Painter, 1828-1874. Arthur Lucas. Illustrated. *Imperial 4to. £3 3s. net.*
One Hundred Masterpieces of Painting. With an Introduction by R. C. Witt. Illustrated. *Second Edition. Demy 8vo. 10s. 6d. net.*
One Hundred Masterpieces of Sculpture. With an Introduction by G. F. Hill. Illustrated. *Demy 8vo. 10s. 6d. net.*
A Romney Folio. With an Essay by A. B. Chamberlain. *Imperial Folio. £15 15s. net.*
The Saints in Art. Margaret E. Tabor. Illustrated. *Fcap. 8vo. 3s. 6d. net.*
Schools of Painting. Mary Innes. Illustrated. *Cr. 8vo. 5s. net.*
The Post Impressionists. C. Lewis Hind. Illustrated. *Royal 8vo. 7s. 6d. net.*
Celtic Art in Pagan and Christian Times. J. R. Allen. Illustrated. *Second Edition. Demy 8vo. 7s. 6d. net.*
"Classics of Art." See page 14.
"The Connoisseur's Library." See page 14.
"Little Books on Art." See page 17.
"The Little Galleries." See page 17.

General Literature

Some Books on Italy.

A History of Milan under the Sforza. Cecilia M. Ady. Illustrated. *Demy 8vo.* 10s. 6d. *net.*

A History of Verona. A. M. Allen. Illustrated. *Demy 8vo.* 12s. 6d. *net.*

A History of Perugia. William Heywood. Illustrated. *Demy 8vo.* 12s. 6d. *net.*

The Lakes of Northern Italy. Richard Bagot. Illustrated. *Fcap. 8vo.* 5s. *net.*

Woman in Italy. W. Boulting. Illustrated. *Demy 8vo.* 10s. 6d. *net.*

Old Etruria and Modern Tuscany. Mary L. Cameron. Illustrated. *Second Edition. Cr. 8vo.* 6s. *net.*

Florence and the Cities of Northern Tuscany, with Genoa. Edward Hutton. Illustrated. *Second Edition. Cr. 8vo.* 6s.

Siena and Southern Tuscany. Edward Hutton. Illustrated. *Second Edition. Cr. 8vo.* 6s.

In Unknown Tuscany. Edward Hutton. Illustrated. *Second Edition. Demy 8vo.* 7s. 6d. *net.*

Venice and Venetia. Edward Hutton. Illustrated. *Cr. 8vo.* 6s.

Venice on Foot. H. A. Douglas. Illustrated. *Fcap. 8vo.* 5s. *net.*

Venice and Her Treasures. H. A. Douglas. Illustrated. *Fcap. 8vo.* 5s. *net.*

Florence: Her History and Art to the Fall of the Republic. F. A. Hyett. *Demy 8vo.* 7s. 6d. *net.*

Florence and Her Treasures. H. M. Vaughan. Illustrated. *Fcap. 8vo.* 5s. *net.*

Country Walks about Florence. Edward Hutton. Illustrated. *Fcap. 8vo.* 5s. *net.*

Naples: Past and Present. A. H. Norway. Illustrated. *Third Edition. Cr. 8vo.* 6s.

The Naples Riviera. H. M. Vaughan. Illustrated. *Second Edition. Cr. 8vo.* 6s.

Sicily: The New Winter Resort. Douglas Sladen. Illustrated. *Second Edition. Cr. 8vo.* 5s. *net.*

Sicily. F. H. Jackson. Illustrated. *Small Pott 8vo.* Cloth, 2s. 6d. *net*; leather, 3s. 6d. *net.*

Rome. Edward Hutton. Illustrated. *Second Edition. Cr. 8vo.* 6s.

A Roman Pilgrimage. R. E. Roberts. Illustrated. *Demy 8vo.* 10s. 6d. *net.*

Rome. C. G. Ellaby. Illustrated. *Small Pott 8vo.* Cloth, 2s. 6d. *net*; leather, 3s. 6d. *net.*

The Cities of Umbria. Edward Hutton. Illustrated. *Fourth Edition. Cr. 8vo.* 6s.

The Lives of S. Francis of Assisi. Brother Thomas of Celano. *Cr. 8vo.* 5s. *net.*

Lorenzo the Magnificent. E. L. S. Horsburgh. Illustrated. *Second Edition. Demy 8vo.* 15s. *net.*

Girolamo Savonarola. E. L. S. Horsburgh. Illustrated. *Cr. 8vo.* 5s. *net.*

St. Catherine of Siena and Her Times. By the Author of "Mdlle Mori." Illustrated. *Second Edition. Demy 8vo.* 7s. 6d. *net.*

Dante and his Italy. Lonsdale Ragg. Illustrated. *Demy 8vo.* 12s. 6d. *net.*

Dante Alighieri: His Life and Works. Paget Toynbee. Illustrated. *Cr. 8vo.* 5s. *net.*

The Medici Popes. H. M. Vaughan. Illustrated. *Demy 8vo.* 15s. *net.*

Shelley and His Friends in Italy. Helen R. Angeli. Illustrated. *Demy 8vo.* 10s. 6d. *net.*

Home Life in Italy. Lina Duff Gordon. Illustrated. *Second Edition. Demy 8vo.* 10s. 6d. *net.*

Skies Italian: A Little Breviary for Travellers in Italy. Ruth S. Phelps. *Fcap. 8vo.* 5s. *net.*

Printed in the United States
136093LV00003B/91/A